CARDINAL BERNARD GRIFFIN

Cardinal Bernard Griffin.

CARDINAL BERNARD
GRIFFIN

ARCHBISHOP OF WESTMINSTER

by

MICHAEL DE LA BEDOYERE

Editor of the "Catholic Herald"

SALISBURY SQUARE · LONDON

Printed in Great Britain at
THE PITMAN PRESS, BATH

CONTENTS

ILLUSTRATIONS

INTRODUCTION

I T SHOULD be made quite clear that this brief study of the life and work of His Eminence Cardinal Griffin, sixth Archbishop of Westminster, which I have been asked to write, is an entirely unofficial work only embodying the views of the writer.

At the same time, I must acknowledge that, such as it is, I could never have written it without the help of those who know the Cardinal far better than I do. Among these I must name in the first place the Cardinal's devoted private secretary, Monsignor Derek Worlock, who has been good enough to furnish most of the unique pictures from his own collection. Among others, I would like to thank the Cardinal's brother, Dom Walter Basil Griffin, O.S.B., Monsignor Joseph Vincent Healey and Canon William Flint for the help they have been willing to give me. But none of these kind friends must be held responsible for anything that appears in these pages.

M. B.

I

THE CALL

THE world was entering its fourth winter of war. The shortening days did not allow of any relaxation of military effort. On the contrary, the country was buoyed up by the certainty that the hour of victory was approaching. The Luftwaffe had long been defeated, and the longer nights only meant an intensification of the raids on Germany. Already one of the Dictators had fallen, and Italy had become a field of successful battle, turning to deadlock near Cassino where St. Benedict's monastery of peace, encircled by great armies, seemed to symbolise the predicament of religion and civilisation in a world in flames. Not far to the north lay the Eternal City, whence Pope Pius XII, on whose shield was pictured the dove of peace, repeatedly called to the nations to curb their savagery, and where he expended himself night and day in helping to relieve suffering, mental and physical. Would Rome itself, would the Holy Father, be involved in the bitter fighting, many were anxiously asking. Far away in the Middle East, and unknown to the people, the Allied leaders were planning together the mighty offensive that from west, south and east was to throttle the empire of Hitler and bring liberation to a new world. Nor did the people know that with three match-sticks it was demonstrated on the "Big Three's" table how easily Communist Russia could annex half Poland, how easily Poland could annex a slice of

Germany. The Atlantic Charter was already, alas, well smudged with the blood of victory.

World war involves, among other evil effects, the disruption of the communications which bind together the different parts of the Catholic Church and which, above all, bind them all to its Head, the Vicar of Christ. In England in that hopeful year, 1943, two Catholic sees had become vacant. In March, the see of Westminster had become vacant when the venerable and beloved Cardinal Hinsley died at the age of seventy-eight. In June, Bishop McNulty of Nottingham died. Catholic sees are filled by the choice of the Holy Father himself after advice has been duly laid before him through the appropriate channels. Happily, a little less than a year before the war broke out, an Apostolic Delegation had been established in Britain, and among the duties of Monsignor Godfrey was the tendering of advice to the Holy See when new bishops had to be appointed. Catholic sees are rarely filled with great expedition, and with wartime conditions and the devious and indirect means of communication entailed, it was not expected that a successor to Cardinal Hinsley in by far the most important diocese of the country would be named for many months.

However, late in November of that year, 1943, a letter sealed with arms of the Apostolic Delegation made its way to North Wales, where Monsignor Williams, the Archbishop of Birmingham, was packing up ready to return to his see after a brief holiday. His secretary handed him the letter. The Archbishop unsealed the envelope, read the letter, and returned it to its envelope without saying anything about its contents. Instead, he asked if the bags were packed and ready. They set off at once.

That evening in Archbishop's House, Birmingham, Monsignor Williams asked his secretary to ring up his auxiliary bishop, Monsignor Bernard Griffin, and find out whether he could drive over from Coleshill, where he lived, for a talk. "And suggest to him that he might care to bring over his things and spend the night." Monsignor Griffin understood. He had received a similar letter.

The Auxiliary Bishop had arrived and had been closeted with his Archbishop for some time. The secretary was then called in and asked whether it was possible to send a telegram so late to the Apostolic Delegation. Yes, it could be telephoned. The text of the telegram was about as short and as cryptic as it could be. It was: "Coleshill agrees. Griffin." The secretary, who could hardly help guessing what it was all about, was chaffed by the Archbishop and warned of the secrecy of such information. Monsignor Williams perhaps need not have been so careful, for the secretary's guess, had it been revealed, would have been wrong. Monsignor Griffin had evidently been nominated to the vacant see of Nottingham, he thought. It never crossed his mind that it could have been Westminster.

We have no evidence of the state of mind of the Auxiliary Bishop when he heard the news, but we may make a shrewd guess that he was more surprised—indeed dumbfounded—than anyone else. And to surprise must have been added a sudden pang of regret, for the great office meant leaving the country of his own people, of his schooling, of his busy, restless, fruitful, apostolic and administrative twenty years of labour as priest and bishop.

It is only a hundred miles or so from Birmingham to London, from Coleshill to Westminster; even so London was a distant, unknown place to a man whose every day had been energetically filled with the manifold business of his own people, of his own diocese. Certainly, he was doing the work of three men, as we shall see; it is said, moreover, that his promotion involved the filling of eleven jobs. In such conditions, one knows and loves one's field of work, and the rest of the world is inevitably a long way off. We need not be too surprised to learn that within a few days the nominated Archbishop was to take twenty minutes to find his way from Victoria Station to Archbishop's House, a London fog having forced the prelate about whom all Catholic Britain was talking to leave his car in Acton and make his own way to the see of Wiseman, Manning, Vaughan, Bourne, and his old superior in Rome, Hinsley. These were all great names: Wiseman, romantically sprung from an Irish-Spanish alliance, with the tradition of Ushaw guiding the transition from a penal past towards the Second Spring; Manning, choosing under the impulse of grace the new Westminster rather than the ancient, exiled Canterbury; Vaughan, of ancient stock, incredibly handsome, the man moulded, it seemed, to the great office; Bourne, a Londoner, already experienced in the rule of a great diocese covering half London; and Hinsley, providentially called in his old age from St. Peter's itself to symbolise the toughness of the nation imperilled and to fight to keep that toughness allied with Christian justice.

Such a lineage of Cardinal Archbishops would be calculated to cause quavering in the bravest heart, called to follow on, and doubts in the wisest and most experienced veteran faced with those responsibilities. For a provincial auxiliary bishop of forty-four it was a giant step.

But the telegram read unhesitatingly "Coleshill agrees", for the new Archbishop was representative of a type of man and a type of priest whose instinct—to put it vulgarly —is to get on with the job. By temperament and by spiritual training he was a man who knew how to obey and, because he knew how to obey, knew how to accept the responsibilities of command—quick summing up, quick decision, quick action. Many must have been the wise heads that nodded meaningfully when they heard that an 'unknown' was to be the chief of Catholics in this country. But, maybe, they had not reckoned in their wisdom on certain facts discernible at much higher levels.

This was 1943 when deeper minds were already concerned with the terrifying problems of rebuilding a world on the divisions and ruins of ideological war—ruins not only to the material order of civilisation, but to the minds of so many who had been engaged in the work of destruction; who had been under the long strain of fighting and waiting, of separation from their families; who had been fed by the propaganda of revenge. And yet they nursed a great hope, one in fact which had been expressed by the Pope in his 1942 Christmas pronouncement when he insisted that in a new society the rights and dignity of the human person must, above all, be defended: the rights of the family, not least in respect of proper living conditions; the proper relationship between home, school and work; the family living wage; the opportunity for fuller education; the right to work.

But could the building of a new society be successful when the unrestrained passions of war had weakened still further the sense of common interest and purpose between nation and nation, between man and man? Within a few days the Pope would speak once more for Christmas, 1943, and he would say: "We see only a conflict which degenerates into unrestricted and unrestrained warfare, as if it were the Apocalyptic expression of a civilisation in which ever-growing technical progress is accompanied by an ever greater decline in the realm of the spirit and of morals."

In fact, the complex technical problems of harnessing to human progress and welfare the scientific resources developed under pressure of war would have to be solved, and solved under the conditions of spiritual and moral chaos in international and social affairs that are the fruit of hatred, revenge and the violently conflicting ideological demands of men who have lost their moral certainties.

To meet such an enigmatic, dangerous and technically complex future, special men, new men, would be required. It would not be a time for great oratory or even great personality. It would not be a time for the generalisers and the intellectuals; it would not be a time for the old aristocracies, but for a new one. One would rather put one's faith in the self-made men who knew ordinary life from within, the men of experience and training, the technically competent, the hard workers, those whose values were deep and sane, and who were not to be dazzled by utopian visions and yet not to be depressed by the slowness and difficulty of real progress.

In a post-war world it would be desirable that a new Archbishop of Westminster, the new leader for Catholic Britain, should have sprung from the heart of the generation of two wars and the first abortive peace, and have shared its experience, its disappointments and its hopes. It would be good that he should be, in the widest sense, a worker—a doer, rather than a talker or a critic. He would need to understand the practical workings of modern social life, not merely be an observer of them, so that he could play a constructive part in adapting that life to fresh conditions. He must know from within the workings of a world wherein spiritual rights and values have to be defended. Such a man would know how to speak the right word when there was still time and not waste a thousand golden words when it was too late. Technique and experience are soulless things when there is no understanding and sympathy with the individual within

1 With Archbishop Williams at Lourdes for the ex-servicemen's pilgrimage, 1934.

2 Bishop Bernard Griffin with his twin brother, Father Walter Basil Griffin, O.S.B., and his elder sister, Sister Mary Philip, on his consecration day, 30th June, 1938.

3   Auxiliary Bishop of Birmingham and Vicar General.

4   The Church of the Sacred Heart and Saint Teresa of the Child
    Jesus, Coleshill, built by Bishop Griffin, 1939–1942.

the mass. To have learnt to feel with others through having shared with them instead of patronising them—this would be needed too. And yet there must be a wider horizon which comes from long and deep study of the doctrine, moral teaching, experience, and values of the Church, so that the trend of events or the practical problem could be instinctively assessed in terms of what is right, what is just, what is true, what will wear well, even though it may not seem immediately attractive or showy. But behind and above all this there must be vocation, the love, the dedication which spiritually warms the practical and administrative actions and decisions of an experienced ruler so that these are not merely so much business, however wise and efficient, but the expression of a spirit nurtured in the apostolic call, in prayer, in the direct service of God whose inspiration alone can give real meaning and direction to human feelings, counsels and purposes.

Let us consider, then, how far the Pope's choice of a provincial auxiliary bishop for the great see of Westminster towards the end of the second world war was justified by the life and work of Monsignor Bernard Griffin, titular Bishop of Abya, and Auxiliary of Birmingham.

II

THE MAN

BERNARD WILLIAM GRIFFIN was born at
7 p.m. on 21 February, 1899, in Oakfield Road,
Cannon Hill, Birmingham. With him was born
a twin brother, Walter. The father, William
Bernard, was a cycle manufacturer's manager, and his
mother was Helen Swadkins.

The Griffin family belonged to those parts and had
been Catholic at least for some generations. They had been
farmers. There was farming stock also on his mother's side,
but his mother's father was not a Catholic. Only in the last
generation or two had these agriculturalists moved to the
rapidly growing industrial city.

The family's religion still retained some of the old
traditions of strong inner piety, protected from a non-
Catholic environment by four strong walls. But just as men
of initiative were moving from the land to the city, so
old-fashioned Catholics were thinking of lowering religious barriers and expanding. It was a district in which
Catholics were few and far between, but increasing in
numbers, and the Griffins were closely associated with the
birth and development of the parish of the English
Martyrs, Sparkhill. There is a ringing English Catholic
sound about it all within the non-English Catholicism of
the country generally.

The family, and the children especially, owed much,
as is so often the case, to a holy and understanding parish

priest, Father O'Hagan. The twin boys, deeply devoted to one another, evidently made a strong impression on the priest. One day they went to confession, and of each Father O'Hagan asked the question: "What are you going to be?" When they came out, the brothers told one another that they had both answered: "I want to be a priest"—and they shook hands on their common purpose. Though Father O'Hagan lived to see one of them a bishop and the other a professed Benedictine, it was early days yet. From the Dennis Road school, the boys gained scholarships to King Edward's School where, with Bishop Ilsley's permission, they received their serious schooling between the ages of twelve and fifteen. Bernard was clearly destined to do very well in all scholastic studies, though, like many naturally clever boys, he would as soon devote himself to games.

Securing a Catholic secondary education was not as easy then as now, though one may hazard the view that a future cardinal did not suffer from the experience of contact with the outer world of a great Grammar School. But scholastic ability and the desire to become a priest were the gateway to a kind of education more in keeping with the traditions and ideals of the Griffins, and in September, 1913, Bernard Griffin went north to Cotton College in Staffordshire. Here he found himself full in the tradition of the great Midland Catholic revival under Bishop Milner which perhaps explained the Catholic generations of Griffin. Cotton, founded at Sedgley Park in those early days—it claims to be the oldest Catholic school foundation in these Islands since the Reformation—had also been enriched by memories of Faber and the Oratorians. The priestly vocation was now shaping itself in that beautiful, wooded, hilly countryside wherein so many monuments of nineteenth-century Catholicity are to be found. And it looked like being an outstanding one, for Bernard Griffin was habitually first or second in his class, thereby, we are told, earning many free days.

But the shadow of war and the holocaust of the coming generation had halted destined courses in England, and in 1917 the twins, still devoted to one another, sought commissions together through the Inns of Court O.T.C. Owing to defective eyesight, his brother was not accepted. Rather than proceed alone, Bernard preferred to go with his brother into the Royal Naval Air Service, commissionless. They served together in the Orkneys, where they were made miserable by the impossibility of getting to Mass. Moved to Manston, Kent, they could get to church, but it meant a four-mile cycle ride in every sort of weather.

Bernard's health broke down. He caught the famous 1918 flu'. He was offered a discharge from the Fighting Services—but refused it, lest it should make it impossible for him to enter the seminary. He recovered, and entered Oscott in January, 1919, where the pang of separation from his brother, who went to Douai, and the difficulties of living the seminary life after the freedom of the Forces were to some extent compensated for by the fact that Monsignor Parkinson was the Rector. For Monsignor Parkinson was an eminent authority on Catholic social teaching for which the student of twenty, with his experience of the world in wartime, must have had a special taste and aptitude, if we are to judge from his subsequent career. Oscott, even more than Cotton, is a shrine of English Catholic history, and no one can live beside the many hundreds of historic pictures, under the jewelled light of the stained-glass coats-of-arms of English Catholic families, near the museum with its many ecclesiastical treasures, without a vivified awareness of what lies behind the English Catholic heritage of to-day.

5 Administrator of Father Hudson's Homes, Coleshill, 1937–1943.

6 With some small members of the family at Coleshill, 1943.

7 Air raid warden at Coleshill in the second World War.

There Bernard Griffin did his course of philosophy. But for the outstanding student Oscott points to Rome, and Father O'Hagan, still watching over those two early vocations, made sure, by applying to the Archbishop, that the English College in Rome would bring to a brilliant realisation the vocation he had first noted so many years earlier.

In the English College in Rome the relationship between England and the Eternal City stretches back 1,200 years. The college was established 400 years ago in its present status as the second in antiquity of all the foreign colleges in Rome, which have come so well to unite in spirit and learning the priests of the Catholic Church all over the world with the see of Peter. No Catholic can fail to be moved even by his first sight of Rome, and we must attach much significance to the fact that so many English bishops in present times have drawn from the English College the long-blended inspiration of Rome and Catholic England. Bernard Griffin went there with Joseph Masterson, later to succeed Archbishop Williams in the see of Birmingham, thus founding a friendship in which both men found strong mutual support, not least in the times when they were called to suffer—the Cardinal for many months; the Archbishop quickly unto a tragically early death. The Rector of the English College was none other than Monsignor Hinsley, and under him studied a veritable nursery of future prelates, Griffin, Masterson, Heenan, Ellis, Rudderham, Grimshaw, Halsall—men whose training together under a saintly Rector, later to be Cardinal-Archbishop, and whose mutual friendship and understanding gained in those days of priestly formation would later serve England well in a united Episcopal Bench.

As at school, so in theological training, Bernard Griffin had little difficulty in absorbing what he was taught, and he moved more easily to his Gregorian Doctorate of Theology while at the English College and his Appolinare Doctorate of Canon Law (taken with Monsignor Cicognani, now Apostolic Delegate in Washington) while at the Beda than he had moved into the respective houses; for, when he first reached Rome, Monsignor Hinsley in his gruff way greeted him with the words "You blackguard!" as the College was full. He received the same greeting four years later when it was a question of studying for the second Doctorate. On this second occasion, he had to be given refuge by Monsignor Mann, the Rector of the Beda.

So, from 1922 to 1927, the future Cardinal received in the Anglo-Roman traditions, and brilliantly absorbed, the technical ecclesiastical training that is necessary for the priest of whom much is expected. Half-way through that training—on 1 November, Feast of All Saints, 1924—he was ordained priest, and the judgment of his old friend, Father O'Hagan, was vindicated.

But behind the arduous studies, there lies something deeper and more important for the true priest: the spiritual development that must give life to the dry bones of learning and give apostolic purpose to the divine power of the priesthood. It was during those years that the future Cardinal imbibed by the grotto of Lourdes and in the Carmel of Lisieux a spiritual depth and simplicity which, as we shall see, has governed his life in good times as in bad. And we shall be right if we leave these years of formation in the rich Anglo-Roman tradition with the picture of the young priest of twenty-eight, kneeling by the tomb of Cardinal Merry del Val, St. Pius' half-English Secretary of State, and meditating on the words inscribed before him: "Da Mihi Animas".

But young Dr. Griffin, newly returned to his native Birmingham in 1927, was not to have his prayers for direct apostolic work for souls immediately answered. He did not go to a parish, but instead to Archbishop's House where his gifts and experience were put to fuller use in the strenuous and perhaps rather thankless job of serving as secretary to Archbishop McIntyre, now seventy-two and nearing his retirement.

He was now on the lower rung of an almost inevitable climb up the ladder of ecclesiastical promotion for a priest of his stamp. Drawn from an established and fervent Catholicism of Birmingham, belonging to the young and hopeful world of light industrialism which made his native city and district the growing centre of Britain's wealth and strength, having profited from the varied experiences of different kinds of schooling, and mixed with all kinds in and after the war, a brilliant student in Rome and one whose spiritual seriousness was known, Dr. Griffin could not have been long in showing at archiepiscopal head-quarters qualities that meant that all this background would yield unusual fruit.

The present writer may be permitted to describe here a memory that has always remained vivid in his mind, even though the incident occurred a few years later when Dr. Griffin had become Monsignor Griffin, Auxiliary Bishop. It was an occasion when a Catholic rally, whose precise nature is forgotten, was taking place in Leamington. It was preceded by luncheon at the local presbytery. A minute or two after the present writer had reached the house, a car swept by. The driver stood (apparently) on his brakes. The checked car swung sharply into the drive, and with a visible rock stopped dead. Out stepped immediately the driver, Monsignor Griffin. In that little, but surely characteristic, incident was illustrated the spirit, the energy, the decision, the youthfulness, even the sense of rhythm and enjoyment with which, no doubt from the start, the new archbishop's secretary faced and tackled the ever-mounting work that was to be thrown on to such willing shoulders.

The Griffin tempo in the thirties of the future Cardinal's life can perhaps best be conveyed by a litany of quickly succeeding and doubled and even trebled jobs. Under Archbishop Williams who succeeded to the see in 1929 and from the start placed the utmost confidence in his secretary, posts of Diocesan Chancellor, Vicar-General, Administrator of Father Hudson's Homes, Chairman of the Diocesan Youth Council, member of the Warwickshire Educational and the B.B.C. Religious Advisory Committees, Director and active worker in the Catholic Evidence Guild, Auxiliary Bishop (in the rapidly developing diocese with new tasks and needs automatically imposing themselves on the man who could most quickly and most efficiently attend to them), even Air-Raid Warden —he was one of the first men to enter ruined Coventry— bewilder the would-be biographer, but were taken as normal by this indefatigable worker. One may judge that the weight of work would have been beyond anyone not endowed with enthusiastic energy, an utter idealism, and above all the power—attested by all who knew and worked with him—of quick judgment, quick summing up of any problem in terms of experience and unusual memory, and quick, almost immediate, decision.

On some of these tasks we may dwell an instant, because they build up the picture of the man who was judged to be the right successor to Cardinal Hinsley towards the end of the war and for the problematic days of rebuilding peace.

A Diocesan Chancellor has to do with thankless, difficult, highly personal and by no means attractive problems of marriage difficulties and entanglements. It would not be easy to find a better field in which to study one side of the truth about human nature. To it all Dr. Griffin gave himself with that sincere interest in individual problems (even, on one occasion, going to the length of buying furniture to save a home) that was always the other astonishing facet of his ability to gobble up administrative work.

We shall not exaggerate in giving (respectfully) the name of 'maids of all work' to those who have to carry out the duties either of a bishop's secretary or of an auxiliary bishop. Constant displacement, constant helping, constant organising, constant correspondence—the continual burden of the second in command to whom the fresh job, the awkward problem, the last-moment emergency can be allotted. But what a school for becoming past-master of the intricacies and responsibilities of modern ecclesiastical administration and rule!

Then the Catholic Evidence Guild—that new type of apostolate in which the priest and the layman discover together how all that has been learnt of Catholic doctrine fares at the hands of the passing, semi-interested, man in the street. The problem of the conversion of England, of Christ's call to go out and teach all nations, is brought down to earth with a vengeance in Hyde Park or the Birmingham Bull Ring, where Dr. Griffin, encouraged by Father Hugh Pope, O.P., one of the founders, would find time to be a regular speaker. Here too was effected a most valuable contact with the growing lay apostolate that must play an ever greater part in the work of the Church in modern times. Friendships made in those days, as with Frank Sheed and Maurice Burns, later Mayor of Hornsey and member of the Middlesex County Council, together with the constant relationship of a priest in Dr. Griffin's many rôles with both Catholic and non-Catholic men in positions of social responsibility, prepared the way for Westminster when the Cardinal would be called upon to deal daily with every sort of person, from the highest to the humblest in the land, Catholic, non-Catholic and those who fall into no category at all.

But for many, surely, the picture that lingers longest and with most pleasure from those days is the one of the priest and bishop in the midst of the children of the Father Hudson's Homes, Coleshill. In any case, exceptionally young in appearance and cheerful in temperament, he looked and was utterly at home with children who instinctively see through any suggestion of patronising or acting on the part of grown-ups. Dr. Griffin's beaming smile, which has never left him, even in times of heavy trial, is the smile of the boy within the man, within the priest, even in the bishop, which has been pictured again and again in the midst of children radiantly happy in his company.

He was appointed to Coleshill as parish priest and administrator in the summer of 1937, and—surely in a characteristic sense of fun—promptly 'phoned his solicitors to see about leaving his earthly affairs in order. Three previous administrators of the Homes had died in quick succession! The solicitors' work could not have been arduous, as he took up his new appointment with five pounds in hand.

The work had been started in the 'sixties of the last century by the Sisters of Charity of St. Paul, an order that had come from France and has since perhaps become better known as the "Selly Park" sisters because of their Mother House in Birmingham. Later Cardinal Griffin was appointed by the Pope 'Protector' of the order. This Cardinal-Protectorship of an order is a very rare privilege, and we believe that Cardinal Griffin is the first English Cardinal ever to receive such an appointment. To this day, it is the

Selly Park sisters who look after the material needs of Archbishop's House, Westminster.

In 1899 Father Hudson had been appointed parish priest of Coleshill. It was his enterprise which built and developed the 100 acres of buildings and grounds which have so long been devoted, under the care of the sisters, to the upbringing and education of boys and girls who for one reason or another have been deprived of parents' care. The work developed on such a scale (it now houses some 700 people—children and those who look after them) that it required three completely separate communities of nuns, with three Reverend Mothers, to deal with the hospital and the different needs of boys and girls, infants and older children. When Dr. Griffin was appointed to Coleshill in the summer of 1937, the year before being consecrated Auxiliary Bishop to Dr. Williams, he was also taking on the administrative side of child and social rescue work whose boundaries were the diocese rather than the Homes themselves. Bishop, Vicar-General, Administrator of the Homes and of all Diocese Youth work—and this at a period when the increased social conscience about all forms of social work, the conditions of war, and the increased diocesan work due to the gradually failing energy of the archbishop of a rapidly developing diocese, heaped on to one pair of shoulders labours that properly demanded half-a-dozen.

Yet his drive and energy were such that despite the threat of war, its outbreak and the consequent hopeless conditions for carrying on the enterprise of his great predecessor who had given his name to the Homes, not Coleshill only, but other parts of the diocese as well, owe to Bishop Griffin new buildings, new works and the first planning of schemes the need for which he foresaw. It is a long and detailed story of vision and patient labour to keep

Catholic welfare a model for the whole district and properly articulated into the developing national organisation which since the war has taken such a revolutionary turn.

Perhaps it is easiest to judge the scale on which Bishop Griffin worked by the single achievement of a vital Catholic need at Coleshill which also was to be a monument and memorial to the work of Father Hudson. Coleshill needed a new church and, given the size of the Homes, it had to be an immense one as compared with the old church across the road or indeed with most Catholic churches in this country. Bishop Griffin tackled the job a few months before war broke out in 1939. When war did break out he lost his architect, who joined the Forces, and his contractor went bankrupt. Nor was the building of churches considered a national priority—anything but! Yet by 1942 the present enormous and handsome church with its characteristic rugged square tower was opened for worship. Its second dedication is to St. Teresa of the Child Jesus, and we need not enquire further about the name of the saint to whom the Bishop prayed for help and in whose hands he entrusted the seemingly impossible enterprise. Indeed, this achievement must be virtually unique in the whole country.

It was suggested above that the new Administrator's action in settling his affairs before succeeding quickly dying predecessors was more in play than in earnest. Yet it may be that there was some subconscious foresight in it, for it is difficult not to believe that the early and severe breakdown of Cardinal Griffin's health may have been due in part to the herculean labours of the years in which he so utterly spent himself for the diocese, for the development of its social work, and, not least, for the children to whom he was the most popular and helpful of fathers.

The reader, we hope, is now in some position to judge

8   Enthroned sixth Archbishop of Westminster, 18th January, 1944.

9   The Honorary Chaplain (R.C.), R.N.V.R., visits the Fleet at
    Portland, 1948.

10 With the Forces
    in Malta, August,
    1944.

of the reasons why the Pope at the end of 1943 chose an 'unknown' provincial auxiliary bishop to fill the vacant see that officially carries with it the presidency of the whole hierarchy of England and Wales and, unofficially, makes its archbishop the head of the Catholic Church in this country.

Of the future, no one could say very much except that it was going to pose great problems, international, national and social. The Pope selected to face them, whatever they might be, a young bishop in the flower of health and energy; one equipped through brilliant studies in England and Rome with the fullest understanding of Catholic doctrine, history and law; a prelate quite outstanding for his age for the breadth and depth of his experience, in every department not only of ecclesiastical administration, but of practice in the intricacies of Catholic social and educational work, the benefits of which could not but greatly count in the work that lay before him in the revolutionary aftermath of a terrible war; a man—and surely this counted at such a time—who had shown again and again that he was ready to tackle, and to tackle with success, anything at all that was put before him—endless, heaped-up, hard work, so far from deterring him, seemed only to whet his appetite for more; and, finally, a Catholic and a priest, who in his upbringing had enjoyed the price-less benefits of a good and intimate home circle, in deep affection for his twin brother, and sisters, one of whom had become a nun, an affection manifested later in his intimacy with fellow-priests, with lay people, and, above all, with children—that key test of a man's unselfishness and spon-taneity—and who had given many earnest signs of the spiritual dedication which underlay his religious, priestly and episcopal vocation.

III

THE ARCHBISHOP

THE new Archbishop, whose Bull of appointment was dated for 18 December, 1943, travelled by car, as we have seen, from Coleshill and Birmingham, where he was so well known and loved, into a London pea-soup fog. From Acton he had to make his way by underground to the bleakness of wartime Archbishop's House. In the train he had been mistaken for the Archbishop of Canterbury and been given a cigar to encourage him! The night before he left Coleshill, he went through the dormitories of the Homes to say his personal good-bye to each of the children, and in doing so he must have felt that he was saying good-bye to all that had been closest and most personal to him through forty-four years of boyhood, manhood and priesthood, lived so fully, so joyfully and so fruitfully. Yet one hesitates to think that he was in any way deterred by the greater unknown wrapped in that fog, or by the darkness of an untenanted, blacked-out Archbishop's House. If we have been at all right in delineating his character, then the new Archbishop must have possessed the power of closing a chapter without repining and facing so formidable a new one without quailing. "Coleshill agrees." He would carry on as God willed and the Pope decreed, strong in a humility that gives strength because it appreciates that one is an instrument in all-powerful Hands; strong, too, in a natural temperament that meets life as it comes, realising that getting on with the job is far more useful than nervously measuring its size.

He was soon to be greatly encouraged by the warmth with which he was received, so that he could say in his enthronement address in the New Year: "Had I been a native of this great city of London, I could not have received a more generous welcome." London and the south quickly took to their hearts an Archbishop who looked even younger than his age; who from the start would put himself at the disposal of his people by being present on every possible occasion, greeting all with his winning, cheerful smile; who, week in and week out, during the war and after it, never lost an opportunity of putting into words the sober, encouraging, realistic teaching of the Catholic Church in matters domestic and international. The appeal and good sense of his outlook seemed all the greater when others were carried away by extravagant emotions and unrealistic visions which sounded so wonderful until one began to assess the cost in injury to the roots of human nature and to those very principles of freedom and justice in whose name the new plans were put forward.

Characteristically, the family man, the man who had had so much experience of both the merits and the shortcomings of social methods of repairing damage to the family and even of trying to transcend it, in his first address declared: "One of the most pressing needs of the Church and nation in this fair land of ours is a revival of Christian family life, which has suffered through the enforced absence of the father, through the removal of the children from the influence of their parents, and through the absence of the mother from her home during long periods of the day when she is in outside employment. A nation depends for its well-being on sound family life;

therefore we should endeavour to remove all those obstacles that exist to the restoration of Christian family life."

This insistence of the primacy of the family, inevitably broken in time of war and threatened by the reformers who planned a new age in peace, was clearly the key to the new Archbishop's whole social approach—and he was not generalising on the basis of first principles, but speaking from an already rich experience.

"The word 'new' is in the air", he said to a Congress of Catholic Youth shortly after the war. "On all sides we hear of a new age, a new youth, and a new world. But there is nothing new under the sun. Don't be misled by slogans and catch-phrases. I want you to realise that the only new thing that must be built is a new and determined effort to preserve old values. But old values can be summed up in one phrase: the hearth and the home. When I say that the battle is joined between the Church and her enemies I might just as well say that the battle we are waging is a battle for the family."

Views like this expressed with such vigour and so few qualifications—views, we repeat, fed by experience and by what a prelate of his position constantly learns from daily evidence of human miseries, misfits, sufferings—might lead one to suppose that the new Archbishop was essentially a traditionalist, almost an old fogey in the face of the new generation steeled in war and determined on a new deal.

There could have been no greater mistake. He had not lived through wars, depression, phoney peace, without realising how much had to be done to ensure that the quality and opportunity for the solid and successful family were available.

He had not been Archbishop for many months when, after a visit to troops abroad, he said: "The day after war

11 The Cardinal kneels before the Pope to receive the Red Hat on his 47th birthday, 21st February, 1946.

12 Receiving the Pallium from his Holiness Pope Pius XII, February, 1946.

13 At his titular Church in Rome, Saint Andrew and Saint Gregory on the Coelian Hill, February, 1946.

14 Princes of the Universal Church: *left to right:* Archbishop Muench, then Apostolic Delegate
to Germany; Cardinal Suhard of Paris; Cardinal Van Roey of Malines; Cardinal Frings of
Cologne; Cardinal Micara, Papal Legate; Cardinal Faulhaber of Munich; Cardinal Innitzer
of Vienna and Cardinal Griffin of Westminster. Cologne, August, 1948.

15 "The Big Three": with Cardinal Gilroy of Sidney and Cardinal McGuigan of Toronto,
Rome, 1946.

was declared I was passing through the streets of Birmingham just as the factories were emptying, and I watched the young men and women, and the boys and girls, as they passed by. Many of them looked physically underdeveloped, round-shouldered and lacking that sense of *joie de vivre* which one naturally associates with youth." With this picture of the end of a peace he contrasted the men, trained to war: "fine, strong, healthy men, clean living and filled with magnificent Christian spirit". In fact, he wanted to see the radical planning and determination, which the needs of war inspired, operative in peace so that the family, "fine, strong, healthy, clean living and filled with magnificent Christian spirit", could be the pride and strength of the nation; and before the publication of the Beveridge Plan, the Archbishop had already given his list of conditions that would make for the "security of home life on the basis of the Christian social system". They were: decent housing for fair-sized families; work for all and family wages; grants to young couples entering marriage; family allowances; recognition of the rights of parents; home helps for mothers rather than day nurseries for children; medical attention in the home rather than away; co-operation between parents and teachers; parental control over sex education; opposition to divorce and the use of contraceptives; encouragement of religion in the home.

Thus from the beginning the new Archbishop presented to Catholics and to the country generally, in so far as it was prepared to listen, an uncompromising Catholic social doctrine round whose central principles was articulated a programme of practical change and reform which touched at many points the aspirations of men and women, still striving in abnormal conditions to bring the war to an end and to build anew something more like a people's world. But he was certain that the essential Catholic contribution to the common task lay in basing all practical reforms, whether in the domestic, social or the international field, on the nature of man as God created him. "At the present day so many of those natural rights are in jeopardy, so many of them violated, that it is of the greatest importance that we, as Catholics, should know them and should be able to inform our fellow-men of their existence", he told the Plater Club when speaking of the Rights of the Human Person.

But though the Archbishop, from the start, was to make speech after speech, full of applied Catholic doctrine expressed in clear, simple language of common sense, because he was ready to appear everywhere and teach his people, there was all the time another side to his work which naturally did not get similar publicity. Habituated before he became Archbishop to being constantly at work getting things done in association and co-operation with the tangle of local authority, with men of importance and responsibility whether in the official or business world, he found no difficulty in applying to the level of Government and Parliament so valuable an experience backed by the ease with which he could mix with ministers, generals and officials of every kind. He well understood that, vitally important as principles are, the practical business of living and getting something concrete done largely depends on person to person understanding and bargaining.

This constant (and unsung) work behind the scenes, carried out with the fullest frankness on his own side and yet the realisation that something gained was always better than nothing, was in fact to earn him the friendship of ministers and politicians of all parties. And this friendship in its turn opened to him a world where the feeling and pulse of events could be measured.

Time and again when he was present at great receptions and banquets he would seize the occasion to have a private and valuable word on some important matter with a minister or official too well protected by secretaries to be easily accessible at other times. Occasions of this kind have inevitably left memories and lessons of interest and value. His lively mind has not forgotten, for example, a Dorchester Hotel dinner on the night of the General Election results in 1945, when near him on one side was seated an old Tory politician and on the other a younger man from the ranks destined to be given ministerial office in the new Labour Government. The contrast between the older person's dismay, as the results flowed in, and the younger one's rough elation was no bad introduction into the new age.

Unfortunately, the first vital business which met the new Archbishop after his accession was one which had already taken its main shape, the Butler Education Bill of 1944. The Archbishop's feelings on the subject were clearly expressed in his enthronement address. "Catholic parents throughout this land", he said, "have publicly insisted on their rights to have their children educated in schools which will not offend their consciences. Whilst others are satisfied with the proposals of the Bill, we Catholics are not satisfied. As loyal members of the State, and as tax-payers equally with others, our parents claim that they should not be allowed to suffer because of their consciences, but should be granted equal facilities with other members of the community."

It was the new Archbishop's view that a major and controversial measure of this kind should never have been introduced in wartime under a National Government which precluded a strongly interested minority from fighting its cause under normal Parliamentary conditions. The question, naturally, directly affected the whole hierarchy,

and the new Archbishop's task as President or Chairman
of the Board of Bishops, older and more experienced than
himself, was to help in ensuring one mind and one tactic
to secure the best possible terms for Catholics. The Archbishop put his trust as usual in St. Teresa of Lisieux for the
cause that all Catholics had so much at heart.

In his position at Westminster, the Archbishop was in
closest touch with Catholic members of Parliament and
he derived much help throughout the proceedings from
them, notably from Mr. Stokes and Commander Bower.
He was present himself in the House for the second reading
debate in February; but of the final issue he had to say "We
have not received justice, nor have our full claims been
met". How right he was has lately been demonstrated by
ministerial admission that Section 76 of the Act, on the
rights of parents, has no binding force.

Cardinal Griffin's continuous dissatisfaction with an
Act of which he only saw the finish was expressed on more
than one occasion later.

At the centenary celebrations for St. Mary's Training
College, Strawberry Hill, in June, 1950, he said; "I entered
the negotiations when most of the main details of the Act
were already in being . . . The 1944 Act was described as
'The Children's Charter', but it really only dealt, as far as
the denominations went, with children who were actually
at school. It took no account of the new generation which
has arisen after the war. It was a hotch-potch sort of Act.
Finally the bishops of the country agreed to give it a trial,
on the understanding that it was not a full solution of their
problems."

Earlier in the year, at the Albert Hall protest rally about
the schools, the Cardinal told something of the inside story
of these negotiations, the first he had tackled at Government level: "Let me tell you how Ministers of the Crown

introduce new legislation. When they know that a new Act will prove offensive to any section of the public they do not usually wield a big stick. With a great show of reasonableness they seek to persuade that section that all will be well if only it is patient. I break no confidence when I tell you that in 1944, the President of the Board of Education, Mr. Butler, and his colleague, Mr. Chuter Ede, told me and my fellow-bishops in conference that they understood our great difficulties. They told us that we should give the Act a fair trial. They told us that if we found it quite impossible to meet the requirements of the new Act we always had the remedy of an Amending Act. That was true. That remains true. There is always the possibility of an Amending Act. There have, in fact, been already two Amending Acts to the 1944 Education Act. Need I tell you that on both occasions the Act has been amended in the favour of the Ministry?"

The shadow of the Catholic schools has fallen on the whole tenure of office of the Cardinal, and we should mistake his mind very much if we thought that he has ever given up the struggle for justice. But, ever a realist, the Cardinal was determined to counterbalance an unsatis-factory deal by starting Central Schools' Funds for raising vast sums for the building of schools which Catholics believe should have been provided by the State. One way or another he was determined on the thing that finally mattered: the existence of completely Catholic schools for Catholic children, and this, thanks to the appeals and pooling of resources, he is getting. Never has there been more building in the Archdiocese than at the present time.

One has insisted that it was always characteristic of the man that he measured up automatically to the size of the job which he was called upon to do—and then, within the limits of his responsibilities, did the work of two or three men in it. Nor did he think it necessary to put in a long period of probation and looking around. His way was always an all-embracing summing up and quick decision and action, after prayer and the entrusting of the task to the guidance of his beloved St. Teresa, whose Autobiography, by the way, was then and has remained ever since his one book of spiritual meditation every morning for half-an-hour before his Mass. So now in his position as the leader of Catholics in the country at war he felt the obligation to go abroad, first, to meet the Holy Father now that Rome had been entered by the Allies, and, second, to be with our Forces. Like other Londoners, he had shared the danger of the doodlebugs. A fragment of one had entered Archbishop's House, and in Millwall when the Archbishop was visiting Catholics in the East End, he narrowly missed being killed.

In the summer of 1944 when all efforts were being concentrated on the liberation of France, it was no easy matter to arrange a journey, even for the Archbishop of Westminster, but happily a quickly struck-up friendship with the Minister of Information, Mr. Brendan Bracken, cleared the way—albeit a roundabout one. The first of dozens of subsequent flights was from Westminster to Rome, via Lisbon (where the next-door plane was due to start for Hitler's capital), Algiers, Rabat and Naples.

The seal on his new work and responsibilities was set when, at length, he knelt to receive the blessing of the Holy Father from whom the Church on the Allied side had been so long separated. Nor are we surprised to learn that the Supreme Pontiff, borne down by the anxieties and labours of "this most terrible of all wars", found in the youthful and cheerful Archbishop, straight from long-resisting, heavily bombed, wartime London, a veritable tonic.

The Archbishop continued his way, speaking to the troops, right up to the front line in Florence, where he was near enough to see German troops and almost near enough to see Cardinal Dalla Costa, the city's Archbishop—in fact, a military chaplain crossed the military lines to take a message from Archbishop Griffin to Florence's Cardinal. This journey enabled him to meet and make friends with Field-Marshal Alexander.

At home, the new Archbishop's immediate contact with refugees from many nations, so many of them Catholic, was a constant reminder of the rights and freedoms which looked like being threatened rather than safeguarded. The Yalta Conference had taken place on the morrow of his accession to Westminster, and it brought the first open threat to the ideals of the Atlantic Charter and the Four Freedoms which faithfully represented the Archbishop's own ideals for a just peace, as they represented those of his great predecessor and old rector at the English College.

One of his first concerns was for the persecuted Jews, and in reference to the persecution of Jews in Hungary he gave the assurance that "any measures taken to alleviate the sufferings of the Jews meet with my full approval". But in this early period the Archbishop's sense of justice was inevitably mainly concentrated on the fate of Catholic Poland. Despite many misgivings, he, like others, had no option but to hope and pray that part at least of Poland would again be free. But by March, 1945, he was already giving the warning so widely repeated since by others: "There would appear to be no word in Russian for compromise", and as news grew worse, he redoubled efforts at least to make the lot of Poles who had found refuge in this country and had fought in the common cause some compensation for their treatment in their own country. Catholic archbishops are poor men, but he did not hesitate to subscribe personally no less than £1,000 to start a fund in answer to an appeal by the Catholic Council of Polish Welfare. As Archbishop and as Cardinal, he has never thought kind words were enough in support of a needy cause. He would work hard for it behind the scenes and, if at all possible, give help in kind.

By the following year, between VE Day and VJ Day, the Archbishop declared that Poland was not free. "The Polish elections will go down in history as a mockery." "The whole political and social life of Poland is, in fact, though not in name, under the closest control of the Soviet authorities and the dreaded NKVD." Central Europe, he saw, was becoming "a Western extension of Soviet power. Europe will be divided into two blocks with disastrous consequences for future world order."

Thus, in those months of leadership at Westminster before the world war was ended, Archbishop Griffin, new to the responsibility and even to London and certainly without having remotely expected such a promotion, put in a formidable amount of work, the detail of which in its many aspects cannot even be touched on here. It must be enough to sense the courage, the energy, the breadth of mind and interest with which he tackled and initiated big problems and seized big opportunities, while devoting himself ceaselessly to the spiritual, moral, administrative, ceremonial and pastoral tasks which fall on any bishop of a large diocese, and which in Westminster mean an endless round of meetings, speeches, visits, contacts, both secular and religious.

But we must record some at least of the words he used in connection with those two great days, the ending of the war in Europe and its complete cessation three months later. "The destruction of war", he said on VE day, "is unprecedented. A great part of Europe is but a shambles.

We are faced with the immense and almost superhuman task of feeding starving people, of rebuilding homes, of rehabilitating families and of making provision for millions of people who have to return to their homes and countries." How much he himself was to do behind the scenes to repair the wreck and save so many of the wrecked he himself could hardly have foreseen. When, in his own cathedral, he appealed: "Let everyone who is listening to me make a solemn promise that in his own sphere he will see that justice is done to those who have struggled throughout these long years of war", he was only asking for a pledge that he himself was destined to carry through to the utmost of his powers during the years to come.

We can to-day take special notice of his words that "the Christian conscience has been shocked by the revelation of recent scientific discoveries which would make war even more terrible", just as we can but lament over his prayer that China "be free to pursue her peacetime activity and develop her ancient culture".

IV

THE CARDINAL

THE ending of war restored normal life to the
administration of the essentially international
Catholic Church which suffers so deeply when
nations are cut away from one another by conflict, and one problem was obviously outstanding. The
Sacred College had been heavily reduced with the years,
and it was expected not only that the Holy Father would
take an early opportunity for restoring its numbers but
that the ever more vital life of the Church across the face
of the world would be reflected in the creation of cardinals
from many nations.

Since the restoration of the hierarchy in England, every
Archbishop of Westminster has been created a cardinal,
three of them some ten years after accession, but Cardinal
Vaughan and Cardinal Hinsley within a shorter time. The
new Archbishop of Westminster was only forty-six—too
young, possibly, for the Red Hat; yet the rôle of Britain
and the Commonwealth during the war suggested to many
the likelihood of his nomination.

Speculation came to an end on 23 December, 1946.
Cables from Rome announced the early elevation to the
Sacred College of thirty-two prelates. At the time, Archbishop Griffin was, as usual, busy. Visiting the sick, as was
his custom, in the Hospital of St. John and St. Elizabeth, he
was one of the last to know that his own name was in-
cluded in the list. Attempts to inform him from Arch-

bishop's House were met by a curt reminder that he was occupied. When he was able to ring back, the line was continuously engaged. He returned in due course to his home to find that a red biretta had been tactfully placed on his desk, and to hear his appointment for the first time from the six o'clock B.B.C. news.

When the newly nominated Cardinal went to Rome for the Consistory, he found that some Vatican officials appeared not to be altogether sound in their international understanding, for it had been arranged that Cardinal McGuigan of Canada should be bracketed with the American cardinals for the receipt of the *biglietto*, or official notification of the creations, while Cardinal Gilroy was being given a Far-Eastern classification. It was Cardinal Griffin who quickly repaired this damage, so that the three new Commonwealth cardinals received their *biglietti* together in the Venerable English College on 18 February.

In his "biglietto" speech Cardinal Griffin stressed the universal nature of the Church, and the necessity of a sound moral basis if true peace and order were to be restored. "This is no time for building castles in the air, or on the shifting sands of expediency."

Three days later, on his forty-seventh birthday, 21 February, Cardinal Griffin received the Red Hat, the Pope embracing him with the greeting "My beloved Benjamin".

He was particularly happy in having been allotted the title church of San Gregorio on the Coelian Hill, like Cardinals Manning and Vaughan, the church of the Apostle of England which has been called the cradle of English Catholicity. He had prayed to St. Teresa for this favour, and, unbeknown to himself, the British Minister to the Holy See, Sir D'Arcy Osborne, though a non-Catholic, had secured the choice for the new Cardinal of England.

These great ceremonies and this close contact with the

Holy Father had deeply impressed Cardinal Griffin with the special mission of cardinals who were princes of the Universal Church. The Pope had specially encouraged him to think in terms of this universal mission, and from this time onwards he was to regard it as a clear duty of his great office to travel abroad and play his part to the utmost in helping to forge Catholic international ties, understanding and practical co-operation.

We have seen how, soon after his accession to Westminster in wartime, Archbishop Griffin was determined to embark on this mission of linking together again the broken ties of the Church. And no sooner had war ended than he—not yet a cardinal—undertook, with the help of the Foreign Office, a journey across liberated Europe: France, Belgium, Holland, Germany and Berlin itself.

In Paris he found Cardinal Suhard engaged in a retreat with 300 of his clergy, the main intention of which was "the restoration of contact with the hierarchies of other countries". The first answer had not been long in coming.

Needless to say, Archbishop Griffin could not visit France without going to pray at Lisieux to the saint who had opened so many paths for him and whose protection he needed more than ever now for the settlement of European problems and the conversion of Russia which lay at the heart of any true future peace. He was in fact the first foreign visitor to enter the Carmel after the war. He said Mass in the infirmary where St. Teresa died, and after meeting her two sisters, Sister Geneviève (Celine), aged seventy-nine, and Mother Agnes (Pauline), the Prioress, aged eighty-three, together with the community, he had a long personal talk with Mother Agnes alone. We may be permitted to believe that this conversation was to have a considerable influence on the different phases of his varied life.

From Paris, he flew to Brussels where he met the exiled Cardinal of Poland, Cardinal Hlond, and in Malines he was the guest of Cardinal van Roey. From Belgium to Holland, where there was so much Catholic resistance to German occupation, and where he met Archbishop de Jong soon to be nominated Cardinal with himself. In Tilburg he was greeted with the British National Anthem by Dutch Mill Hill missionary students. In this journey he could see for himself the devastation caused by modern war and the size of the problem of reconstruction and resettlement. But it was only when he drove from Utrecht to the British Military Headquarters in Herford, Germany, that the true measure of war's horror and the task of reconciliation through practical help and relief was seen to be overwhelming.

In Munster he found the courageous Bishop von Galen, also soon to be Cardinal, living in the utmost simplicity, and it was arranged for the English Archbishop to preside at Bad Driburg, near Paderborn, over a meeting of the German bishops of the British Zone. The Archbishops of Cologne and Paderborn and the Bishops of Aachen, Berlin, Hildesheim, Munster and Osnabruck attended. One pressing problem was that of Catholic education, and the German bishops were thinking in terms of the Concordat system. But Archbishop Griffin suggested the more satisfactory pre-Concordat arrangements—Catholic schools for Catholic children with Catholic teachers. Said Bishop von Galen: "I have fought the Germans; unless it gives us our schools, I will fight the British Government too." Dr. Griffin shook the anti-Nazi prelate by the hand and said: "I shall do the same."

The Archbishop of Westminster had been greeted by the northern bishops as the bearer of the olive branch of peace. By Cardinal Faulhaber, in the two surviving rooms of his palace, he was greeted as a new Boniface. Once again he had the opportunity of meeting other German bishops and of discussing the future of the country.

All this experience Archbishop Griffin put to very good purpose when he reached Berlin and met the heads of the Military Governments, as well as Miss Ellen Wilkinson the Minister of Education. With regard to the importance of Catholic education in Germany with a view to the building up of a democracy in the country, he was able to press the points made by the German bishops and win the case for the pre-Concordat arrangements for the confessional schools.

With this important and successful mission just accomplished, we can well understand why he appreciated the Pope's insistence on the international mission of a cardinal when he received the great honour, the more so in that the Pope himself told him that Cardinal von Galen had just reported that it was due to the Archbishop of Westminster that the educational question in Germany had been solved along the right lines.

Three months after receiving the Red Hat, the Cardinal was once again carrying out with tremendous vigour the Pope's mission to strengthen the links between Catholics of different countries. In the space of fourteen days he covered 10,000 miles in a journey to and within the United States. During the fortnight, he carried out an average of twelve engagements a day. That is easy to say, but in practice it means a non-stop outflow of energy, of friendliness, of courtesy, with sleep snatched if and when the opportunity offers. On one occasion an engagement could only be kept through the emergency arrangement of a long night journey by car. Loss of a night in bed after gruelling days did not worry him.

The high spot of this tour, which caused Americans to

say that the English Cardinal knew how to out-hustle the Americans themselves, was the reception of the Doctorate of Civil Law (*honoris causa*) at Fordham with the President of the Republic himself, Mr. Truman. Americans perhaps knew even better than Englishmen how to appreciate the English Cardinal's smile and easy friendliness with all, and the reception they gave them made it clear that he was Britain's best roving ambassador in those days.

As the months passed in those critical post-war years when the future was shaping ominously, the tireless Cardinal, ambassador for both Rome and Britain, the ideals of both of which separately, but even more together, he had so much at heart, took every opportunity of travelling, meeting and seeing for himself.

France (he seized of course every opportunity to obtain spiritual refreshment in his beloved Lisieux), across Canada, Denmark (where he was greeted by the King and Queen), Brussels (to receive an honorary degree from Louvain), Cologne (for this seventeenth centenary of the cathedral), these and other long foreign journeys succeeded one another at an average rate of three a year. But perhaps the most remarkable was the journey to Poland in June, 1947 —one so unpopular with the Polish authorities that every attempt was made to delay and hold up his visa until threats of publicity had to be made to extract it at the last hour.

The Cardinal flew via Holland and Prague, where he met Archbishop Beran, and on to Warsaw and Lublin whose bishop was the future Cardinal Wyszynski. Though he missed Cardinal Sapieha, who was in Rome, the Polish Cardinal pointed out that this was the first post-war visit of a foreign dignitary of the Church to Poland. He spoke of how the Polish nation had been moved by the attitude of the English bishops to their suffering country. "Cardinal

Griffin is a tested friend of Poland. He belongs to those Englishmen who did not alter in any way their cordial attitude towards the Poles and Poland. While greeting him on Polish soil, we honour in him a representative of the Senate of the Church, the primate of Catholic England and a friend of our nation whose feelings do not change." He was not exaggerating, for the English Cardinal had his car on one occasion literally picked up and carried along by the enthusiastic Polish crowd.

From the Polish bishops, Cardinal Griffin learnt at first hand of the increasing threat to that great Catholic country, and of how already its people were being prepared to concentrate and strengthen their Catholic ideals and life within the family where religion could survive longer than anywhere else. We can be sure that this experience of persecuted Catholics confirmed his own sense of the primacy of the family.

We should realise that a visit like this one, coming after all the direct experience of the state of Europe which he had gained through travel, and the immense amount he had learnt at first hand from those from abroad who had written to him, consulted him and begged his help, very deeply affected him as perhaps few in this country could be affected. The human imagination is a limited faculty, and strong as the will may be to sympathise with the sufferings of those we read about and to see justice done, it is only when the reality is directly seen and experienced that human feelings are fully engaged. Hence when the Cardinal, as early as his 1947 Advent pastoral, said: "The forces of evil are gaining ground and threaten to destroy the soul of man, the soul of Europe. Now more than ever we are faced with the dilemma of acting for God or against God", he was not expressing a generalisation, however true, but deep personal feelings fed with the evidence of the reality.

6   Preaching in America: Buffalo Eucharistic Congress, 1946.

[*Acme Newspictures*]

17   Shaking hands with President Truman after both had received an Honorary Degree at Fordham University, New York, May, 1946.

[*Illustrated*]

18   The after-dinner speaker: entertaining Mr. De Valera at the St. Patrick's Night Banquet, 1954.

19 Assisting at Mass at Holy Child Convent, Mayfield, 1946.

20 Presiding at departure ceremony for Franciscan Missionaries of Mary, Farm Street Church,
1952.

In these years, 25 per cent of the Cardinal's letters came from abroad, and a high percentage of these were concerned with personal cases of displaced people, people in prison camps awaiting repatriation, European volunteer workers and others in need. There was an enormous amount of work to be done in connection with the Yugoslavs stranded in Germany, Croats, Slovenes, and others whose whole future lives were in jeopardy according to which side of the Iron Curtain they would be fated or forced to live upon. The Cardinal's efforts in these cases, much of this work being done in co-operation with Lord Pakenham, then in charge of German affairs, must have saved thousands of people from death or slavery, for, but for him, they would have been forced back into Tito's Yugoslavia.

It is against such a background as this that we must measure his feelings as he watched the arms of Communist persecution steadily pressing forward to grasp more and more of the Church and destroy the human liberties which, in the last analysis, will not stand up against the denial of the rights of religion in the schools and in the churches.

Archbishop Stepinac, the first of the great persecuted prelates; Cardinal Mindszenty; Archbishop Beran; Cardinal Wyszynski—these are more than names and more than symbols to a fellow Archbishop and Cardinal who has known them and seen them in the actual context of a continent, first filled with the human suffering that modern war leaves behind it and then threatened, not as an abstract entity, but in the hearths, homes, individual lives, free ways and, above all, free worship and Christian living, of countless human beings. One meets here with a spiritual current of redemptive suffering, fed through so much deeply sympathetic contact with suffering men and women and the suffering Church, that was in due course to bring him to share in his own body and spirit what he had seen and realised in others. The 'laughing cavalier' Cardinal which the public saw was only the outward aspect of a person who had seen and experienced too much in those post-war years not to give new depths to the spirituality he had learnt in the school of St. Teresa of Lisieux. The sequel would show it.

THE LEADER

W E have been swept along in a most inadequate
bird's-eye survey of Cardinal Griffin's conception of the work laid upon him by the
Pope when he created him a prince of the
Universal Church so soon after the war, and when his
years, his natural energy and the broad sweep of his mind
and interests made him so natural an ambassador of the
Church as it resumed in threatening conditions the links so
long broken by war. If the rush of the account suggests
something of the rush of the Cardinal's life, it will not have
been completely inadequate.

But all this, of course, was but a cardinalitial super-
structure to the heavy tasks that faced him at home both
as the Catholic leader in the country and as the Archbishop of the large diocese in which half of London is
situated.

The immediate post-war years were, as we remember,
filled with most important social and administrative discussion and legislation. It may be that Cardinal Griffin,
despite his years of religious formation abroad, had to learn
as he went along when it was a case of fully seizing the
problems of the world at large, but his experience of the
relation of local social administration in Birmingham to
Catholic values and morals had fully prepared him for the
national problems which were now to face him. Here he
was very much on his own ground, and the Catholic

community in Britain was lucky indeed to have him to take care of its interests.

Among the measures of special importance with which he had to deal in those years we can number the National Health Service Act of 1946, with the National Insurance Act, the National Assistance Act of 1948, the Children Act of the same year and the National Service Acts.

Of these by far the most important and difficult from the Catholic point of view was the Health Act because of the question of Catholic hospitals, which numbered more than seventy. The Cardinal, in his position, had obviously no political bias against Aneurin Bevan's great scheme, and in principle, no doubt, he would be in favour of bringing within the reach of all the means of safeguarding so important a human asset as health. Those who have worked for years among the less fortunate sections of the community would not be tempted to think otherwise. But he had already said: "It will be a sad day for England when charity becomes the affair of the State." From the Catholic point of view, health of body and health of soul cannot be dissociated, and it was a formidable thing to face the passing over of Catholic hospitals, staffed by religious communities and created by the pennies of Catholics themselves who wished to ensure through and through the Catholic character of the places where they might need spiritual administration most.

Happily in Mr. Bevan the Cardinal found an adversary capable of establishing a relation of personal friendship and frankness on both sides. Indeed, the Minister of Health was an admirer of Catholic hospitals, not least the great London hospital of St. John and St. Elizabeth. This, of course, was not necessarily an advantage, for he wanted that hospital in particular for his national scheme. The discussion between them to reach a solution satisfactory to both sides—

and this meant, from the Catholic point of view, the retaining of the full denominational character of the Catholic hospitals—lasted a very long time. The struggle went on to the end of the debates on the Bill when the Cardinal considered that Catholic interests would not be sufficiently safeguarded by the House of Lords amendment to maintain the denominational character of Catholic and similar hospitals. The Cardinal had only one last card to play. The whole hospital system in this country depends to a considerable extent on the recruitment of Irish nurses. That recruitment might well be jeopardised if there was an open fight on this question between the Catholic community in these Islands and the Government. Mr. Bevan was shrewd enough to appreciate the finality of the point, and he had to give way. The Catholic hospitals were on the list of disclaimed hospitals, and it was thanks to the Cardinal that such hospitals, Catholic or otherwise, were enabled to opt out. Those who knew the whole story were saying that the Cardinal was the first person to get the better of Nye Bevan.

The National Insurance Act raised complex questions about the position of priests and nuns within the system. It needed the Cardinal's attention and help to work out a solution satisfactory to all concerned. Many other than Catholics owe it to Cardinal Griffin that in the National Service Act of 1947, theological students were deferred from National Service up to the age of twenty-five, owing to their studies—and by that age they were usually ordained.

The Children Act, which provided for the care and welfare of children who for one reason or another cannot be under the care of parents, was of course a field in which the Cardinal's experience in rescue work in Birmingham and Coleshill made him an authority. The Act followed the Curtis Report.

The Cardinal, commenting on the Report and its criticisms, vigorously defended the work that had been done for "forgotten children" especially those under Catholic care. "The aim and object of voluntary societies has been to try, as far as is humanly possible, to make up to the child its home life and the affection which it should have had from its parents." He mentioned the names of Cardinal Manning, Cardinal Vaughan, Monsignor Hudson, Father Bans and Father Berry who "began the work of looking after what were, in those days, the waifs and strays. For the most part, our care of these children has been committed to nuns who have made it their special vocation. It is not their custom to defend themselves when attacked nor to speak of the invaluable work they have done over long periods of years in very trying circumstances." Turning then to the importance of this work, the Cardinal, who had so often defended the home as the basis of a good society, very characteristically showed how this kind of care, properly done, is better than a bad home. "We have to insist that the ideal foster home is also one in which the foster parents are of the same religious belief as the child." And when he said that many children's Homes to-day are often better built and better equipped than good boarding schools, he knew that that was the case where he himself had laboured. "We have not yet reached the high standard of our ideals nor do we claim perfection. But we do know that anyone who has the work at heart will continue to make progress with the one thought in mind—the welfare of the children."

Another Act of special interest to the Cardinal was the National Assistance Act which, among other things, aims to provide more adequately for the disabled and aged. His social interest, which is in fact the application of his Christian love for his neighbour, covers every human need, and just as one of his more recent pastorals has been devoted to the care of the aged, so earlier he would especially praise the devotion of nuns to this work in the spirit of the Church, adding bluntly: "We do not resent direction or inspection provided it is done in a spirit of constructive help and not by private or bureaucratic busy-bodies." One suspects that one of the banes of this 'professional' in social and indeed other problems is the busy-body and the untrained amateur, though his courtesy would never allow him to show it to the individual.

Once again, in connection with this subject, the present writer can personally vouch for the fact that the Cardinal is not one of those social workers who believe that one's Christian duty is fulfilled by promoting someone else's good work or charity. He believes that such money as he has at his disposal is meant to be circulated, and he does not wait to be asked. If he thinks he sees a need, Catholic, personal, social, he will spontaneously offer some financial help if he possibly can. This, alas, is by no means a very common quality in human nature.

A bishop so conscious as Cardinal Griffin has been of the practical problems of the contemporary world—problems in the natural, technical and social order which need to be solved if the supernatural itself is to find its God-intended setting—would inevitably pay a special attention to the importance of Catholics playing their full part as citizens and as Catholics in the world of to-day, and specifically in the world as it is lived and run in the traditions of their country. The nature of the Christian influence in public life and citizenship has often been insisted on by the Cardinal in very practical terms, for he knew what he was speaking about. "The Public Assistance Committee", he said in the course of a very detailed speech on an official visit to the mayor of Finchley, "does not merely exist to dole out relief, but the members ought to be inspired with the charity of Christ, and have a strong personal interest in the poor. Some of the institutions in which the poor are housed are a disgrace to this nation. Why should not the aged poor be provided with comforts and amenities such as are enjoyed in a normal home? . . . If the work is being done by Christian people, they will provide nothing but the best. One would hardly imagine that a Town Planning Committee had need of Christian principles to guide them, but new houses and even flats that have to be erected should not make it impossible for married couples to bring up a normal family. Even the Assessment Committee must frame its decisions on justice and equality."

In the same speech, the Cardinal was, no doubt, thinking of Birmingham experience—after all, his own father had been a member of the Birmingham City Council—when he said: "I am a firm believer in local government because it seems to me that in it we have a true expression of democracy and liberty. The bond between those who are governing and those who are governed is much more intimate, and local needs will be better understood and more easily dealt with by local authorities than by direction from Whitehall."

It is easy to generalise on the proper relations between Christian principles and public life, but the disciple of Monsignor Parkinson and the bishop so long experienced in local affairs, and now constantly dealing with national ones, not only liked to go into details, but to be ever active in seeing that religious and moral principles were more than barren abstractions in his own country, and that scientific, technical and social advance was directed towards ends consonant with the true, God-made nature of man. To further this, he would always encourage Catholics to play a full part in national life.

[*North London Press*]

21 The civic round: being received by the Mayor of Hornsey, Alderman Maurice Burns, March, 1955.

22 The eternal autograph: with film stars Kathleen Ryan and Stewart Granger at Pinewood
Studios, 1946.

23 Throwing in the ball to start a Gaelic football match, Mitcham Stadium, 1947.

24   With Father Peyton during the Family Rosary Crusade, July, 1952.

"To-day I want to tell you of your duty, as Catholics, to set an example of good citizenship", he wrote in a Lenten pastoral. "But I do not want you to think that this is not a spiritual message . . . It is easy for us to forget that spiritual duties have an immediate bearing upon our lives in eternity . . . It is necessary, at a moment when international and political rivalries [it was in 1948] tend to disgust honest men and lead them to renounce active interest in public affairs, for our Catholic people to be instructed in the nature of their civic responsibilities."

In the same pastoral, he emphasised the need for Catholics "to take an active part in the affairs of local or national government". "As Catholics," he insisted, "we have a great deal to offer . . . The Catholic, from the reading of the social encyclicals, has a sound knowledge of the mutual duties and responsibilities of the family, the State and the individual. Problems of education, matrimony, the social and medical services and the rights of the workers—to give a few examples—are bound to recur with regularity in every public assembly." And he urged Catholics to join the Catholic Social Guild so that they could contribute constructively. As we have hinted before, the Cardinal has little use for the mere theorists and the generalisers. They can do more harm than good.

Because of this concern for a full and informed Catholic contribution to professional and political affairs, he has rarely missed an opportunity of personally guiding and encouraging Catholics to play their full part, and he has done this not in a negative spirit of only warning against dangers (necessary, these days, as this has been) but of positively encouraging. Thus, for example, talking to Catholic delegates to the British Medical Association Congress in 1948, the Cardinal prefaced necessary warnings with the charming and helpful words: "Priest and doctor have very much in common. We both deal with human beings. We are both concerned about their welfare, you mainly about their temporal welfare and priests mainly about their eternal well-being . . . You are there at the beginning of life and so are we. You are present when men are sick and so are we. Very often both doctor and priest meet together at the sick bed and are with the patient when he is breathing his last . . . I always think that we are both moved by the same desire to help others who are in need of our help and that we are inspired with the same divine charity."

Whether talking to Civil Servants, industrialists, teachers, soldiers, nurses, writers, it is always the constructive opportunity, the *vocation*, which the Cardinal likes to emphasise, and in doing this the necessary warnings which he gives have a fuller and more encouraging meaning. Thus, in an address on 'The Church and Industry in Derby,' the Cardinal said: "I should like then to speak of work as a vocation . . . surely every work can be a vocation since God has destined us to work . . . The very work upon which I am engaged is the very instrument of my salvation and hence for me it is a matter of extreme importance and, indeed, of immense value."

Active Catholics in this country are organised in a number of societies or associations, not for the purpose of trying to insert the Church into public and professional life, but for the purpose of encouraging and instructing Catholics to play a more useful part as citizens in the affairs of the world and the country, and in order to make them spiritually and morally conscious together of their Catholicity. In this country there has never been any serious suggestion, for example, of forming a 'clericalist' political party, and nothing could accord more with the Cardinal's own feelings, as his own temperament is anything but 'clericalist' in the usual sense of the word. The Church in the contemporary world has to act in that 'mixed' field where morals and politics and administration meet, and no one has been more forthright in seeing that legislation will not be tolerated that runs counter to the natural law or in raising his voice where injustice and hypocrisy rule in the field of international affairs. But he greatly prefers *not* to have to act or protest, believing and praying that good-will, common sense and technical resources will suffice, and hoping that bishops, priests and the laity will be able to contribute necessary Catholic action *from within* rather than *from outside* the work that has to be done. Thus one can find the ideal in this field, as the Cardinal sees it, in organisations like the Association of Catholic Trade Unionists, the Association of Catholic Managers and Employers (both of which were founded in Westminster under his leadership and encouragement), and the Young Christian Workers (to which he has more than once given most positive approbation) as well as the Catholic pro- fessional guilds.

At the foundation of ACTU, the Cardinal expressed his pride in British social legislation, and stated the proper aims of the Association—and we may safely take them as representing accurately his own ideal: "First and foremost to assist and encourage Catholic workers to join their appropriate trade union . . . Secondly, to assist and en- courage Catholic trade unionists to take an active and personal interest in the trade union movement in general and in their own branch in particular . . . Thirdly, to safe- guard Catholic interests of Catholic trade unionists in the trade union movement. And, finally, to induce and assist Catholic trade unionists in the trade union movement." When the Catholic Managers and Employers' Association was inaugurated two years later, the Cardinal's realism forced him to admit that "all is not right in business and commercial transactions here at home", but he saw practical ways in which Catholic employers can make a positive difference. Anything is better than nothing for a man who has had long experience of how to fight for something, at any rate when you cannot get all.

Some may say that no very spectacular success has attended this practical and realistic outlook, and in particular some may think that such Catholic societies would be more successful if organised on a national, rather than diocesan, scale. But the Cardinal has always preferred the bird in hand to two in the bush. Like any other leader with high authority and at the centre of things, he has in the long run to depend on the vitality and keenness of followers. If this is not sufficiently forthcoming on the diocesan level which is within reach, why should it miraculously appear when at the national, and more diffused, level? The essential for effective Catholic organisation, he believes, is that the work should take root in the parishes—the ground floor, as it were.

Moreover, as we shall consider later, a very considerable progress has been made during the Cardinal's years at Westminster in making Catholics more generally conscious of their opportunities and the country more generally conscious of the importance of the Catholic body. And this (one may be permitted to surmise) has been due in no small measure to the quality which corresponds with a realist determination to gain real victories where they can be gained rather than plan for utopia, namely a tremendous respect for personal freedom, initiative, vitality. One has heard him say of enterprises with which he may not wholly agree: "At any rate, it has life." And there can hardly be any bishop more ready to hear and be genuinely interested in other people's points of view, more easy to talk to, slower to take offence—slower even to resort to the sanctions that are inherent in ecclesiastical, or any other, authority and necessary to it. The way of reason, of kindness and of understanding is the way of a prelate to whom men and their God-given freedom and responsibility matter tremendously.

The important field of writing, whether in books or papers, as well as other means of communication, such as radio and television, have always been sympathetically respected by the Cardinal and intrinsically good work, rather than just "pious", actively encouraged. The sense of impish fun which makes him cherish originals of clever cartoons directed against himself is one to tolerate the views, variations and mistakes that inevitably express themselves in work that is alive, though he is ready to raise a voice of caution when he sees any danger of misunderstanding. Catholic newspapers have always found him a friend quick to appreciate good work and ready to smile over less good, and always very reluctant to criticise or get excited over matters that cause nervousness in narrow minds. Under his rule effective public relations have been established for the first time at Archbishop's House.

VI

"IN SICKNESS . . ."

WE now come to a period and an aspect of Cardinal Griffin's life of which one can only treat at a respectful distance because of the personal nature of the subject. But the reader may be assured from the start that in these pages he will find understatement, not overstatement.

One can perhaps date the period best by referring to the fact that, on 25 September, 1948, the Cardinal, accompanied by his great friend, Archbishop Masterson, whom he had had the special happiness of consecrating Archbishop eighteen months earlier, travelled to Lisieux to attend the national celebration of St. Teresa on the next day. He in fact attended the Pontifical High Mass in the basilica, and took part in the procession of the relics of the saint, and stayed in Lisieux for about a week. When he returned to England, the Cardinal preached in his cathedral on the saint and said: "I am convinced that if only we have been able to learn from her the lesson of confidence in Almighty God that we have it in our power to do great things for Him if we will only, like St. Teresa, become as little children in his hands."

Less than two months earlier, the Cardinal had been at Walsingham to receive the pilgrims who from all parts of the country had carried fourteen crosses in penitential pilgrimage to Our Lady's historic shrine. There, before many thousands of people, he dedicated the whole country to the Immaculate Heart of Mary, saying: "The spirit of materialism would set itself up in the place of God. It is the spirit of all that is evil—lying, hatred, deceit. This same spirit of materialism, of the denial of man's high destiny and of his soul and spirit, will reduce man to the position he occupied during those pagan days when Christ came to rescue the world." And the Cardinal ended by referring to prayer and penance at Fatima: "It is the only solution to the problems which face us to-day."

We may recall that the Cardinal came from a family for which the focus was the Catholic faith, struggled for and kept through generations when the Church was still to a great extent a hidden minority—a family such as he him-self was to describe in a Teeside speech this very year: "To us a home has to have a very intimate meaning. It means something sacred—a real home is one where mother, father and children are united in a small independent society." We recall, too, the signs of his own vocation, together with that of his twin brother, to the priesthood. In such circumstances, the spiritual life would be a very personal, a very real, thing that is lived first, and only talked about after. Spirituality is dedication in work—work for God, for the Church, for one's neighbour, for the world.

It is interesting to note how the Cardinal in his sermons and speeches always seems to want to *apply* religion, devotion, the great mysteries and truths of the Church to *practical* action, to the state of the world, to the struggle between good and evil, to greater enthusiasm and competence in the active service of God. In a sermon for Easter, the theme is that of victory over the forces of evil: "No matter how a man may scheme to dethrone God, no matter how great may be the persecution of the Catholic Church, the power of Christ is greater"—and the theme is applied to the work of the Church, no less to-day than ever before, as also to the Catholic family, the Catholic individual, where "great work" can be done "through the power of Christ's Resurrection. It may sound impossible. It *is* impossible, without his help."

In an address to young men preparing to become priests, he stresses the power of the priest to help, as no one else can, for the priest shares in the eternal priesthood of Christ, and in the first offering in the supper chamber and the offering in any parish church, the sacrifice is one and the same.

But in the sermon on the Resurrection we find also: "Christ did not come to offer us a life of ease and comfort. He showed us the royal road of the Cross. He told us that we must become perfect as His heavenly Father is perfect. He gave us high ideals, but He also gave us the grace to live up to those ideals. He summed up His teaching by the two commandments of the love of God and the love of our neighbour—a life of obedience and service." And in the address on the priesthood he said: "The Code of Canon Law says that a priest must lead a more holy life than a lay person and the greatest helps we have, as priests, are the holy Mass and our life of prayer. These two must be intimately connected. If our priesthood is going to be something real and effective we must be men of prayer."

We may here note in parenthesis the Cardinal's tremendous personal interest in the formation and care of the spiritual lives of his own clergy, and the interest he has taken in helping the priest to be a completely dedicated man; as one of the means to this, for him, all-important end, he has set apart his own country house at Hare Street as a place where the priests of his diocese can find regular spiritual and physical refreshment in a manner that perhaps recalls St. Ignatius' insistence that his priests should devote a year of their early ministry to recapturing at a

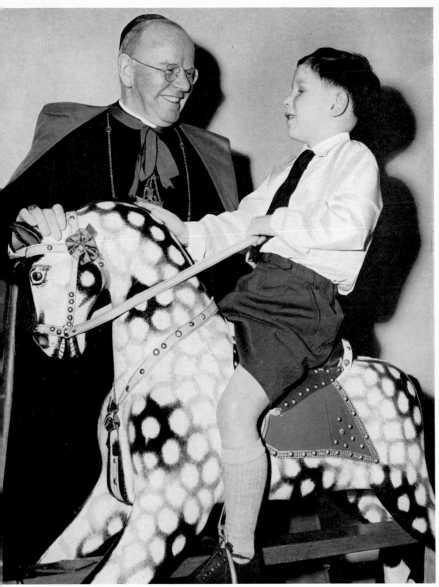

25 Opening the new children's ward at the Hospital of St. John and St. Elizabeth, London,
February, 1955.

26 Helping at a party for orphan children, Westminster, January, 1949.

27 With the children of Niepokalanow, Poland, June, 1947.

28 With Cardinal Hlond in the ruins of Wroclav Cathedral, Poland, June, 1947.

maturer age the fervour of their youth when they elected to
serve God in religion. He has also instituted the Days of
Recollection for his clergy.

We can see then how behind the administrator, the
practical man of affairs, the man who enjoys social contact,
whether on great or quite homely occasions, the famous
and so spontaneous smile, the mountain of activity, there
lies the hidden depth of a simple, perhaps, but completely
dedicated spiritual life in the raising of the mind and heart
to God, who is all, and in the forgetting of the self which is
nothing—the spirituality he had learned from years of
special devotion to St. Teresa and, we may surmise, from
the truths he had the great grace of learning from her
own sisters.

That is why we have dated the coming phase of his life
from his visit to Lisieux, towards the end of September,
1948.

By December of that year the news had come that
Cardinal Mindszenty had been arrested. We have already
noted that from the time of his appointment to Westminster onwards Cardinal Griffin was brought into intimate and unceasing contact with the miseries of war, as he
saw them in his travels and as he continually faced them in
the multitude of letters in which desperate people turned
to him for help. We have seen, too, how those years revealed themselves to him as increasingly critical for both
the Church and the civilised world—how in particular he
had had to watch the enveloping wave of persecution of
the Church of which he was a prince, a Papal counsellor, a
most devoted son; and he had had to watch Catholics
whose lives he had shared, prelates and priests he had met
and with whom he had become friends, hearing the
dreaded secret police knock at their door, and enduring
prison, torture, brain wasting and sometimes death. He had

himself seen the beginnings, as in Poland, of the squeezing
away of Catholic life and allegiance from millions of good,
innocent people, to prevent which we had fought a long
war and which now was performed in the name of victory
over Nazism.

And then came the most significant, the most audacious
act of all: the arrest and trial of his fellow cardinal, elevated
to the Purple with him, Cardinal Joseph Mindszenty.

But at the protest meeting of Catholic bishops and
people in the Albert Hall on 7 February, 1949, the Cardinal-
Archbishop of Westminster was missing. The chair had to
be taken by the Archbishop of Liverpool, Dr. Downey.
Twelve days earlier, the following announcement had been
made: "His Eminence Cardinal Griffin has been suffering
from nervous exhaustion following overwork and has
been ordered to rest for several weeks before fulfilling
further engagements."

Just before he had been taken ill, the Cardinal had been
writing his Lenten pastoral. In it he spoke of St. Teresa and
of suffering: "In suffering there is a deeper meaning still:
not only must we share the pain of the Cross, but we must
learn its redemptive power . . . Borne with patience and
in union with Our Lord, suffering is of far more value than
any penance which we impose on ourselves. Self-imposed
penances are good and necessary. But they carry with
them the danger of spiritual pride. Sometimes they are
selfish and cause others to suffer with us."

We do not know whether those words were written
with any knowledge or premonition of the imminent
breakdown of his health. But the Cardinal certainly could
have had no conception of the nature and amount of
suffering of which, during the next few years, God was to
allow him to become the victim and which, as he certainly
believes, St. Teresa gave him as a spiritual gift that he

might share in the suffering of Catholics and of the world
that he had so closely seen. Through that resigned sharing
he would be given his own full part in "the redemptive
power of the pain of the Cross".

Leaving aside the mystical current about which one can
only guess, together with the psychological and emotional
influence on a person who felt so deeply about the sufferings of others about which he had known so much more
than ordinary people, there is no doubt that the sheer
overwork of the years in Coleshill and the years at Westminster goes far to account for the length and severity of
an illness which was rightly and literally called "exhaustion"
—the absolute rebellion of a body which, we remember,
had been strained while in the Services and which had since
been the slave of a nervous will to eat up the avalanche of
work that can fall on the too willing shoulders of an omni-
capable leader and an efficient bishop. And, returning for
a moment to the mystical current, can one not see a
spiritual link between the nature of an illness that leaves a
man temporarily helpless, denuded of his powers, completely in the hands of nurses and friends ready to minister
to him, and his becoming, as the Cardinal had preached on
his return from Lisieux, "like St. Teresa, as little children
in God's hands?"

The Cardinal was in fact anointed for the first time in
this first phase of his illness, and he spent his fiftieth birthday
in the care of the nuns of the Hospital of St. John and St.
Elizabeth, for which he had so long fought with Mr.
Bevan—a visitor, by the way, to his bedside in that hospital
when a little earlier he had had his tonsils removed.

His birthday, we recall, was also the anniversary of his
receiving the Red Hat at the hands of the Pope, and we may
here anticipate the words of a leading article in the *Daily
Express* two years later, on the occasion of his fifty-second

birthday when he had recovered and returned to the full execution of his duties: "It has been the good fortune of Catholics in the period of social change since the war to have a Cardinal whose special bent is for social affairs. In five years, it is claimed that he has got through the work of a lifetime. To-day, not only Catholics, but people of every religion will rejoice that he is regaining his health."

But there were many weary months to go before that, and inevitably there was much speculation about the sudden illness and future of a Cardinal Archbishop whose most notable characteristics were immense energy, unvaryingly cheerful spirits and readiness to tackle any and every job. The sheer sense of vacuum expressed itself in curiosity as well as deep anxiety. No doubt, this was heightened by a sense of mystery. Usually a severe illness of a high prelate leads to many medical bulletins and organised prayer for his recovery. But it was typical of the Cardinal's spirit that grave illness and deep suffering were just as much part of the picture of God's will and providence as each day's normal timetable. The telegram "Coleshill agrees" remained as normal and inevitable now as in 1943. One may note in passing that the same was true of his lifelong friend, Archbishop Masterson—a tower of strength to the Cardinal and those near him during these months of illness. Archbishop Masterson, who knew the fatal illness which had seized him and could joke about it, allowed himself to die before his clergy and his people were allowed to realise that he was in immediate danger.

The Catholic community remained in suspense until 26 March, 1949, when a bulletin was issued to say that the Cardinal was expected to leave hospital at an early date. A week later, the Cardinal sent a letter to his clergy, in which he expressed his very grateful thanks to "the religious communities, the faithful and the children" for their sympathy and prayers. "Thanks to the devoted care and attention shown me by the doctors and nursing staff of this hopital, I am happy to say that I am making good progress towards recovery." The expectation which he expressed in that letter of an early convalescence was fulfilled on 20 April when he left for St. Leonards. The next official news was that the Cardinal would be able to fulfil his engagements in the late summer.

Typically, the late summer was interpreted by him as mid-July when he was back in his native Birmingham at the annual general meeting of the Catholic Truth Society. There he spoke strongly and sharply about the Government's policy abroad and at home. "It will not be my fault if through shortsightedness the British Government helps to build up tyranny in the East or fails to support the just demands of free citizens at home." The first part was in reference to British trade with persecuted Czechoslovakia. "Cardinal Mindszenty, Archbishop Stepinac and Archbishop Beran", he declared, "are all one in that they represent the Church of God, victimised by Soviet Communism, the most formidable enemy of Christian civilisation in a generation." The second part referred to the Government's refusal at home to do more than coldly state that no new settlement of the education problem could be negotiated in terms as favourable to the denominations as in 1944, in answer to the evidence submitted by the hierarchy demonstrating the wild inaccuracy of the financial forecasts of six years earlier.

Naturally, one of the first desires of the Cardinal, despite the continuance of high blood pressure which caused anxiety about the future, was to pay a visit to Lisieux there to pray to St. Teresa and to give thanks for a recovery that was quicker and fuller than had been at one time expected. So on 8 September he flew to Lisieux, and next morning celebrated Mass in honour of his saint and in thanksgiving in the Carmel Infirmary where St. Teresa had died. He was back in London the same day—a measure of the pressure on his time so soon after an illness due to monstrous overwork.

His optimism, alas, was very much ahead of the facts, and anxieties about persecution abroad and the vital problem of the Catholic schools at home were not calculated to help him. On 23 September it was announced from Archbishop's House that there had been a set-back to the progress he had made, and that he needed further rest and treatment.

Within only a few weeks, on 1 November, the feast of All Saints, the Cardinal would be celebrating his sacerdotal silver jubilee. On that day, he was well enough to preside at Pontifical High Mass in Westminster Cathedral celebrated by Bishop Myers, and to intone the *Te Deum*. Those present were astonished to find him looking so well, but they did not know that the Cardinal was in fact not well enough to celebrate Mass himself on that day of all days for any priest. His recovery, however, continued, and indeed he got so much better that by December, 1949, the Cardinal was virtually in harness again. Indeed, many matters of the highest importance were awaiting his attention.

It was a time when it had become clear that there was little hope of justice, or indeed of the fulfilling of the promises made by Mr. Butler in 1944, where Catholic schools were concerned. It was necessary to make the country know and realise the true state of affairs and the feelings of the Catholic community which, in the Cardinal's own words, "will not keep quiet". To this end a national meeting in London at the Albert Hall and similar meetings in different parts of the country were planned.

Thus at the end of January, 1950, the Cardinal's first public appearance since his illness was at the Albert Hall amid most of his fellow bishops and 7,000 of his own people who took the occasion to express in their reception of the Cardinal Archbishop their feelings of joy and gratitude at having him back with them on this loyal and fighting occasion, and one so suited to the Cardinal's own temperament.

He spoke well and strongly, admitting the vast audience to part of the inner story of the negotiations and declaring roundly: "It is intolerable that we should be regarded as obstacles to progress in education, simply because we refuse to accept a death sentence for our schools."

The Cardinal was present, too, a few days later on the plinth of Nelson's Column in Trafalgar Square in the presence of an immense crowd of praying Catholics who, despite the fact that they had been refused police permission for silent marches from all parts of the capital, were so orderly that the police declared they had never had experience of a crowd so large, and yet so well disciplined.

Cardinal Griffin had declared in the Albert Hall that the Education Act was a "death sentence" for Catholic schools. But the man who disregarded apparent death sentences on himself would certainly not bow before a death sentence on Catholic schools. Despairing of public justice, he was at this time already preparing his plans for a new method and a new system of, raising the necessary monies, namely by Central Schools' Funds which broke through long-established traditions of the past and which many feared would beggar the Church. In fact, everyone, clergy and people, were to respond to his determined spirit and achieve the impossible.

The second great matter demanding the Cardinal's attention and personal leadership at a time when his health was giving such anxiety was the celebration of the centenary of the establishment of the Hierarchy in 1850. This would be an event of unique significance and it would mark before the country and the world a hundred years of Catholic history, life, and progress in Britain—a growth that was coming into full flower during the years following Cardinal Griffin's accession to the see of Westminster and leadership of the Catholic body. But the full commemoration of such a centenary inevitably demanded not only much preparation, but as much of the personal presence of the Cardinal Archbishop himself, as possible, especially once he had been appointed the Pope's Legate for the great occasion.

The Cardinal, however, fell very seriously ill again at the end of July. It was only two months before the great day when the Centenary Congress would draw nearly 100,000 Catholics to Wembley Stadium to greet the Pope himself in the person of his Cardinal Legate.

This time the Cardinal might well be said to have been literally struck down. For two months it seemed to those near him utterly impossible that he could be present in person at Wembley or at any of the other great functions that would mark the Congress. But particularly because he had been nominated the Pope's Legate, Cardinal Griffin was determined to appear. He realised that the Congress itself would have to be postponed if the Papal Legate could not attend it.

The result was an absolutely astounding recovery from the depths of illness—a recovery just in time for him to be solemnly received as Papal Legate in his cathedral, to preach at the Mass for the clergy in the ruins of Southwark Cathedral, to be at the Wembley rally, and to be the principal guest at the banquet at Grosvenor House given by the laity in honour of the hierarchy.

29   The flying Cardinal: arriving with the late Archbishop Masterson and Monsignor Worlock
for the International Eucharistic Congress, Barcelona, May, 1952.

30   Praying for world peace at the International Eucharistic Congress, Barcelona, May, 1952.

31 Visiting the ruins of Hamar Cathedral, Norway, during the Breakspear celebrations, July, 1953.

32   At the Grotto, Lourdes, May, 1953.

Solemn, important and fatiguing as all these occasions were, the moment that must stand in so many memories was the appearance of the Cardinal Legate at Wembley, a sick, limping man, leaning on the arm of an attendant as he slowly made his way to his throne, and then at the end the same Cardinal walking away unaided, his stick carried by the attendant. The cheer which he then received from 90,000 people was unique even in that place of cheering crowds, and it proclaimed the feeling of admiration and gratitude for a Cardinal's immense courage. Yet in that vast assembly only very few had any idea of just how great that courage was in the light of his so recent utter prostration.

The Cardinal's recovery enabled him to keep going and even to fly to Rome, with Archbishop Masterson, for the Definition of the Dogma of the Assumption. In Rome, too, there was amazement at his presence and his insistence on walking up alone to receive the Pax from the Holy Father at the Pope's Solemn Mass after the Definition of the Dogma in St. Peter's Square, a ceremony which the Cardinal had not found himself strong enough to attend.

With the prolongation of his grave and incapacitating illness, there was of course speculation about the future. On this visit to Rome the Cardinal saw the Holy Father, who granted to him the assistance in his work of Bishop Myers who was to be promoted to the rank of Archbishop and 'given to the see' as the Cardinal's coadjutor. With this help, the Cardinal felt, he could carry on in the faith that God had only given him that surprising power of recovery because he was meant to fulfil the duties of his high office. It was "Coleshill agrees" once more.

It is consoling to think that the suffering of those years could at least be alleviated to some extent by rest and happiness under the care of the Sisters on the heights above

Torquay, as well as by the friendship, whether on holiday or on other occasions, of Archbishop Masterson and the devotion of his secretary, Monsignor Worlock.

But the end of the trials which he accepted in all spiritual simplicity as a contribution to the work he could do for the world, the country, the diocese, fully as real as that of his earlier intensive labours, was not yet. At the end of January, 1951, the Cardinal had a severe attack of coronary thrombosis, and for the second time he was anointed. He had to be long in bed and to have a long convalescence, ending once again in the early summer with the peace of Torquay and the special joy he has always experienced when in the company of young children. After this there was no recurrence of the grave and alarming symptoms of the last two years, and this the Cardinal has attributed to the intervention of Blessed Cuthbert Mayne to whom he made a special novena after receiving a relic of the saint from the Bishop of Plymouth.

He himself described what happened when addressing 7,000 pilgrims at Launceston in the summer of 1952 to do honour to the martyr in the largest religious gathering in that county of perhaps all time. "You will know," the Cardinal said, "that in the last few years I have not enjoyed good health, and just a year ago I was in the West Country recuperating from a serious illness. Your Bishop was kind enough to bring to me for a fortnight that precious relic, the martyr's skull. It was my privilege to have it in my chapel during this period, and after the Bishop had blessed me with this relic, we made a novena to Blessed Cuthbert. My subsequent improvement in health has done much to confirm my faith in the heavenly power of this great martyr."

There was indeed no spectacular recovery, but also no looking back, and the Cardinal, though still retaining from those months of suffering a slight limp and an occasional weakness of voice (to correct which he has worked with a recorder and in consequence attained a greater ease and effectiveness of public speaking than when he had no time for such details) has gradually returned to a schedule of activity which, if not what it once was, is more than enough for the healthiest and most active of ordinary men.

He himself would wish us, in closing this chapter, to pay tribute to the skill and devotion of his doctors, Mr. D. K. Mulvany, Dr. P. Corridan and Sir Daniel Davies. The first two, as Catholics, were made Knights of St. Gregory: the last, as a non-Catholic, a Knight of St. Sylvester. And they, we think, would wish tribute to be paid to the courage and cheerfulness of their distinguished patient.

VII

"... AND IN HEALTH"

RECOUNTING the story of Cardinal Griffin's illness and long and courageous fight against such heavy odds, we have been obliged to pass over the significance of those months in the history of the Church in this country—a significance which has become ever more apparent in the last two or three years whose events remain greener in the memories of all of us.

The Hierarchy Centenary Congress served to focus what may well be called the coming of age of post-Reformation and post-Emancipation Catholicity in Great Britain. The Cardinal himself, preaching in Southwark Cathedral said: "From the small beginnings of 1850 so much has come that we clearly see the hand of God in the increase that has been granted. As we look around us at this congregation of clergy, can we not marvel at seeing in this very church more priests present than there were in the whole of England and Wales one hundred years ago. The development for which Cardinal Wiseman and his faithful flock hoped and prayed has been made. We have more churches, more monasteries, more convents, and more schools. Here are the fruits of the labours of those who have gone before . . . Full of confidence, therefore, as they were in 1850, let us go forward, resolving anew to co-operate with the graces made available to us by Almighty God, that we may not prove unworthy in the tasks that lie ahead."

Another aspect of this growth, especially in the last years, was referred to by the Cardinal in 1950 in the course of an address to the Sword of the Spirit. "One thing that has happened since 1940 is that the English people have become increasingly conscious of the Catholic Church as a great force in the post-war world. The minds of our countrymen have changed a great deal since the 'thirties, when the importance of religion, like the danger of atheistic Communism, was underrated or ignored. To-day it is a commonplace to be told by non-Catholics that they fully recognise that in the strength of the Catholic Church, much more than in any purely material resources, lies the great hope of saving Europe, and, indeed, the world."

The Cardinal has in fact been the leader of the Catholics in this country during a period of special danger and of special opportunity.

We have seen how intimately concerned his years of rule have been with the assault on the Church in Europe and Asia, how the enemies of religion have not hesitated to arrest and maltreat brother-cardinals and other leaders of the Catholic people in various countries. Nor can it be denied that in our own country and other freedom-loving countries, these years have shown a growing indifference to spiritual and moral principles with worship and Christian upbringing in family and school steadily decreasing. Yet this persecution and this indifferentism have shown themselves to be an unprecedented opportunity for Catholics to become ever more conscious of their faith and strength and for others to become ever more conscious of the importance of the Church.

Only a few years ago, the filling of the Albert Hall for the expression to the country of the feelings of the Catholic community or to register their mass protest would have seemed a mere dream. To-day, it takes place automatically when the seriousness of the occasion makes the protest necessary, as with the Communist treatment of a Cardinal Mindszenty or a Cardinal Wyszynski, and the demand for tickets of admission is much greater than the number which can be issued.

And who would have dreamt that the Catholic community could fill the immense Wembley Stadium, not only for an historic commemoration, like the Hierarchy Centenary, but for a purely spiritual occasion like the Family Rosary Crusade and the celebrations for Our Lady's Year? Not less indicative of the changed position was the success of the Vocations Exhibition at Olympia, chosen by the Cardinal as the setting for an ordination of thirty priests in the sight of more people than had ever witnessed such a ceremony in this country.

One may perhaps ask how the Cardinal has personally contributed to the Catholic community's new consciousness of itself and of what it stands for in the nation. Cardinal Griffin has not chosen the way of the spectacular leader, the great orator, the intellectual or cultural personality. Some may have regretted this, as they had perhaps mingled regret with their surprise at the Pope's choice of a young, unknown, provincial auxiliary bishop for the great see. But in fact if we look at the evidence, we shall see that Cardinal Griffin has given the country something more valuable and more necessary at the present time.

He has given himself—*all* of himself.

While behind the scenes he has given his keen intelligence and wide experience of administration and technical affairs to labouring for the best possible Catholic status, influence and defence in national affairs, the Cardinal has literally made himself the servant of all—to the most serious breakdown of his own health—in a surely unique way.

A cardinal is a cardinal—to non-Catholics he is one of the highest officials of the universal Catholic Church, the undisputed Catholic leader and responsible executive in the country, the spokesman of the Pope himself; to Catholics, he is all this and much more—he is a spiritual father of unique and eminent dignity in the country, he is the voice and symbol of the millions of the faithful. When such a person really does put himself at the disposal of all, making himself as readily present at the humblest gathering and the simplest occasion as at the greatest and most important; when he as readily mixes with the humble as the great, without acting, without assuming any pose, but just being himself, a friend, a cheerful influence, one who understands and can talk and take real interest, no matter with whom he finds himself, and yet one who can do this without for a moment betraying the dignity of his office and the responsibility of his authority—then, surely, he must all the time be wielding an extraordinary influence which in the aggregate lifts up the whole tone of a community, subtly gives it self-confidence, even more subtly imparts to it a share of his own courage, confidence, spirit.

The trouble about this method of giving oneself, instead of leading with a gesture or a slogan, is that it is killing for the person who does it, not least when the scope of the overwork is not a mere diocese, but a whole country, not a whole country, but a world, that universal world of the Church of which a cardinal is a prince and representative of the Holy Father.

That is why one cannot but view the Cardinal's life from a spiritual angle. His life as Cardinal Archbishop has been in fact a killing self-dedication in an immense accumulation of those little things, upon the importance of which he has meditated daily in following the teaching of

St. Teresa of the Child Jesus. These are little things, not in the sense that they are of no importance, for the responsibilities of a Cardinal Archbishop of Westminster force him to deal continuously with highly important business, but they are made little by the spirit in which they are faced, a spirit of detachment from self and from self-importance, a spirit of complete trust in God. And how obvious has been the value of this, even on a merely temporal level, since it must go far to explain the lovable and helpful qualities he has shown, his simplicity, his personal friendliness and even sense of fun, his very English regard for liberty and individuality, not merely in the abstract, but where it is a case of the views, mistakes, failings of the person with whom he is in contact, his love and regard for life, activity, getting on with the job and his prejudice against too easy theories and generalisations, even, no doubt, a certain impetuosity and quickness of reaction that may prove disconcerting.

And surely we shall only understand the spiritual quality of dedication and selflessness, when in full health, which seemed so natural and even inevitable, if we couple it with his months of illness and suffering. Not only was the first a direct cause of the second, but the second is but another facet of the first in that both are forms of the same detachment from self and attachment to God, according to God's will that his service for Church and country should be expressed by active work or redemptive suffering.

The awakening of the Catholic body to a full consciousness of itself and its complete emergence from that state of siege and privacy characteristic of a nineteenth century Catholic family like the Griffins is not of course an end in itself. "Go ye and teach all nations." "Be ye perfect as your heavenly Father is perfect"; it is these ends of apostleship and the deepening of the spiritual life which,

33   In the Carmel at Lisieux, September, 1948.

34 Recuperating from serious illness: the Cardinal with two of his doctors, 1949.

we may say, have especially marked the leadership of
Cardinal Griffin in these latter years of ever fuller recovery
from his illness.

Cardinal Griffin expressed his mind most fully on this
theme in his Lenten pastoral in 1952.

"To-day", he wrote, "we cannot over-emphasise the
importance of Christians living a full Christian life, a life
that is in accordance with the teaching of Him who is the
way, the truth and the life . . . At no time in the past has
it been more important that the laity should be conscious
of their rôle and adequately trained for their task. Their
apostolate is to be fulfilled as ever under the direction of
those who have received their authority from the Church
founded by Christ. It is for the laity to share in the apostolate of the hierarchy and, if their rôle is dependent on the
hierarchy of the Church, this in no way diminishes the
importance of their task or the very real responsibility
which is theirs." Having explained that the number of
priests has not grown in proportion to the number of
Catholics and that in the modern world there are many
places not easily open to the ministry of the priests, "there
is grave danger", he continued, "that this field of the lay
apostolate may be thought to be closed to all save specialists
and experts . . . The lay apostolate is open to all. It is the
duty of all, irrespective of class or background, to play
their part within the life of the Church. Each apostle must
be trained and prepared for carrying his Christian principles into the very sphere in which he has his being. This
is as true of intellectuals and students as it is of professional
men and women and working youth. The university
professor has a part to play in the life of the Church as
much as has the member of a trade union."

Then the Cardinal returned to his favourite theme of
the apostolate within the Catholic family and within the

boundaries of the parish. But "some will be called to more extensive activities by membership of Catholic societies and organisations . . . in which they will be able both to work for their personal sanctification and also to bring the charity of Christ to their non-Catholic brethren."

Lastly, the Cardinal invited co-operation in the fields which he had made specially his own in his life's work. "We have also urged our people to enter into the civic and public life of the community. Here indeed is a true field for the lay apostle . . . Few are called to extend their apostolate to an international plane. But to those self-sacrificing men and women who devote much time and energy to the fulfilment of the universal rôle of the Church we extend our earnest and heartfelt thanks. More than ever before it is necessary to-day that the peace-giving principles of the Christian faith should permeate the conduct of international affairs."

In the light of the all-embracing sweep of the modern rôle of the lay apostolate, as Cardinal Griffin understands it, we can appreciate better the motives that have prompted him before and after his illness—the interval being scarcely more than when actually stricken down—to be personally present, whenever at all possible, at the meetings of Catholic societies, at public Catholic occasions, wherever Catholics were gathered together in vocational and group form. We can appreciate why so much of his time was devoted to planning, encouraging and directing fresh Catholic enterprise, as with ACTU and ACME; why, in particular, he attached so much importance to universitiy societies and, for example, the establishment in London of a most attractive new university chaplaincy under the direction of so outstanding a priest as Monsignor Gordon Wheeler and later of Monsignor Tomlinson. His appreciation of the importance of intellectual and cultural leadership

in the Catholic body stems from his own early studies
which, had he been called to a different life, would have
doubtless make him a professed theologian or canonist of
distinction in the country.

It was the same desire to encourage the ordinary Catholic everywhere to a sense of his modern opportunities
which prompted him to travel endlessly within the country
and abroad. Since his illness, the Cardinal has not let up on
this determination to 'show the Catholic flag' on important and the simplest occasions and to encourage Catholics
personally, whether it be a rally of cyclists, a charity con-
cert, or a Commonwealth reception. His desire to be 'all
things to all men' has been markedly realised, not only
because of the depth of the spiritual motive, but because
it remains his nature to be just himself in any company, the
same good mixer whether in a palace or a pub. It comes as
a surprise, for example, to learn that in the year 1952, so
soon after his recovery, he visited no less than sixteen
dioceses in the country and made a number of visits abroad,
as though nothing had happened to him in the meanwhile.

We recall a series of days after Holy Week in 1952
before the Cardinal's recovery was complete. After the
long hours in the cathedral for the solemn services of the
season, the Cardinal managed personally to attend Catholic
meetings for doctors, journalists, the Catholic Truth
Society, education, apart from the work of the Low Week
meeting of the bishops. He was present at Tyburn Convent.
And, into the bargain, he travelled to Birmingham and to
Aylesford to keep public appointments.

One may mention here as an excellent example of the
Cardinal's unceasing readiness to work for a constructive
solution of problems as they emerge with the passing of the
years the work he has been doing for Irish Catholics who
have come to this country to obtain the ready employment

that is hard to find in their own country. The number who have thus taken advantage of this country's industrial development in recent years is no less than 800,000. The problem of helping these Irish men and women to settle into this country, of safeguarding their religion and that of their families and of integrating them into the community of their fellow Catholics in this country is inevitably a difficult one. But the Cardinal has given much of his time to it and, in association with the Irish Hierarchy, has done a great deal to solve it. Not an Irishman himself, he has nevertheless won admiration and affection from the Catholic Irish in this country, and when he is seen and photographed throwing the ball at an Irish football-match and being the honoured guest at an Irish reunion, it is well to remember that this is only the outward aspect of a deep interest which covers, behind the scenes, solid labour for the spiritual and temporal good of those who come to our shores.

With a start like this, we can easily guess the pace at which he has since continued. Yet in these latter years the Cardinal's work has, we think, been marked by a certain change. Though action and work have not diminished, one feels that he wishes still more to emphasise the necessary spiritual quality and fervour behind action and work, whether in the individual or the community.

The development of the lay apostolate, always emphasised during his years at Westminster, comes now as a logical development of the fact that the Catholic community has become conscious of itself and grown able to express that consciousness, not only in great meetings in the capital, but throughout the country. And logically following on the beginnings of the realisation of the lay apostolate a renewed emphasis has come, in the Cardinal's words, on "the importance of Christians living a full

Christian life". "Love of God", he has written in a recent pastoral, "is meaningless if it does not also embrace our fellow-creatures . . . But if we are filled with an all-pervading love of God, then this will inspire the first movements of our minds."

That primacy of the love of God as the inspiration and the key of apostolic action has expressed itself in the great nation-wide spiritual crusades of Holy Year and Our Lady's Year; in the drive for a greater number of priestly vocations, focused at Olympia; and in the rapidly growing interest in the historic shrines of the country that was once "Our Lady's Dowry", as well as in the growing devotion to the English martyrs.

Not all these devotional occasions were initiated by the Cardinal of course, but the fervour and enthusiasm with which he has responded to them has not only proved decisive in rallying the whole Catholic people to them, but also caused non-Catholics to be struck by their significance. This enthusiasm seemed to spring inevitably from one to whom the spiritual was always primary and who had now learnt in the school of suffering its supreme value.

Father Peyton had no more keen supporter than the Cardinal, present at the Hyde Park rally and host at Wembley. The suggestion of the crowning of the statue of Our Lady of Willesden, the ancient shrine in his own archdiocese, despoiled by the Reformers, was taken up by him with such enthusiasm that he decided to organise the immense gathering at Wembley which seemed to symbolise the linking of the millions of Catholics to-day in the country across the centuries with their forefathers who made this island the Dowry of Mary.

The cause of the canonisation of English martyrs, centred in the Cardinal's mind on Blessed Cuthbert Mayne proto-martyr of the English seminaries, to whose intercession the Cardinal believes he owes these years of apostolic labour, cannot but stimulate the whole body of English Catholics to look again for spiritual inspiration to the heroes of their own blood and land whose martyrdom was the seed of the restored faith—the faith that is so markedly growing in our own times.

None of this makes the Cardinal any less of a realist. He is well aware of human weakness, of the imperfection of measures adopted, of the time and experience needed for fuller and firmer faith, but others can at least see that if any man is praying and working for spiritual progress, it is he. And probably he himself would place first the work so graphically brought to the attention of the country in the Vocations Exhibition. Concern for the spiritual and temporal welfare of his own clergy, not least through the trying period of war and transition from war to peace, has, as we have seen, always marked his episcopate. And certainly a numerous, devoted and well-trained clergy must always be the rock on which a country's spiritual progress rests.

An important spiritual development of recent years, for which we all have to thank the Holy Father, has been the adaptation of rules of liturgical worship to the contemporary needs of the faithful: the means of enabling the people to participate as a body more intimately and visibly in the Offering of the Sacrifice of the Mass; the change in the Eucharistic fasting laws; the introduction of the Dialogue Mass, the establishment of Evening Mass. These changes, most of which are at the discretion of the bishop, have been eagerly accepted by the Cardinal as helping towards the enrichment of the spiritual life of his flock.

More controversial matters, still largely in the sphere of discussion, such as increasing use of the vernacular, are

35 With his private secretary, Monsignor Worlock, in the Cathedral Precincts, May, 1951.

36 On holiday in Ireland: with Archbishop Masterson at Derrynane, August, 1953.

37 With the author's son, Stephen, at Strawberry Hill, June, 1954.

far from being remote or closed questions in the Cardinal's mind. On the contrary, as the present writer knows from the Cardinal's own words to him, here too he is sympathetic and eager for developments for which the ground has been sufficiently prepared. In these matters, as in so many others, the Cardinal, suspicious of superficial enthusiasms and easy generalisations, always retains a practical and open mind.

Very soon after he came to Westminster, in July, 1945, the great national cathedral of Westminster celebrated its fiftieth anniversary. In it, as the Cardinal put it at the time, "Roman liturgy was joined with English dignity". No archbishop has accepted the unique liturgical inheritance of the cathedral with greater pride, and one of his early decisions was the re-opening of the Cathedral Choir School—also in many ways unique—after the war.

Through the years, the Cardinal has whenever possible taken his place as Cardinal Archbishop in the great ceremonies of the cathedral, and very many must have been the worshippers during those years who have noticed his always recollected and dignified bearing during the rich liturgical pageant, and this even when they wondered at the fortitude and devotion with which he was overcoming the physical weakness of his period of ill-health.

Lovers of the cathedral and of its great liturgical tradition owe to the Cardinal to-day the happy appointment of Monsignor Gordon Wheeler as its Administrator, to carry out his own plans to make Westminster Cathedral the liturgical centre of the country and an inspiration to non-Catholics as well as Catholics.

It is perhaps fitting that one should find in Westminster's cathedral the final setting for this description and study of the Cardinal's leadership and work, as it is being carried on to-day. Standing in the heart of London, its great campanile rises towards heaven, sign and symbol of the whole work of the Catholic Church, of which the Cardinal is leader and spokesman in this country. Within it, prayer is unceasing, to it thousands come in joy or distress, seeking the Eucharistic presence of Christ within a work of man not wholly unfitting that sublime Presence and participating in due worship with the solemnity and beauty that transcends the centuries and the chequered history of humanity.

Cardinal Griffin has dedicated his own life to the work of God which with his dignities and responsibilities covers almost every aspect of social and individual life; but the heart of it all has ever been the deep sense of the presence and service of God in good times and bad, in health and suffering, on great occasions and on more homely ones, in matters of decisive importance and in matters of passing moment. The heart of it all lies in his cathedral.

And since this is an account of a great churchman who, despite illness, remains in his fifties a man of full vigour with, we pray, very many years of work before him, we can take leave of him, as it were, in his own home, Archbishop's House, which stands next to his cathedral.

We may be permitted to see him of an evening when, in obedience to his doctors' orders, he seeks relaxation perhaps in watching the television, perhaps in a novel. Those free evenings are too rare, since public engagements constantly take him out, sometimes to late hours. But they, together with the spectacular change of rising half-an-hour later than he used to, are all that doctors can get out of him in the way of nursing himself.

The habit of relaxing has come to him late in life, for he had no time and no natural disposition to learn the art. Now perhaps on a peaceful evening, when his book is boring or the programme too bad, he can, for the first time, look back—to the happy, vigorous days of childhood

38 Papal Legate to the Hierarchy Centenary Congress: with the Canons of Westminster at the throne in the Cathedral, September, 1950.

39 Leaving Wembley Stadium at the conclusion of the Hierarchy Centenary Congress,
    1st October, 1950.

INTROIBO AD ALTARE DEI

40   Ordaining thirty priests during the Vocations Exhibition, Olympia, July, 1953.

41   Presiding at the St. Boniface Centenary celebrations, Buckfast Abbey, June, 1954.

in a home "with a very intimate meaning"; to the first seeds of priestly vocation planted and nursed by Father O'Hagan; to the memory of Archbishop Williams who discerned his exceptional capacities; to the neat and sturdy house in which he lived at Coleshill, surrounded by the 'unwanted' children who loved him and whom he loved.

Then came the great day when with a two-word telegram he accepted the undreamt-of see of Westminster and the truly red-letter day when Pius XII gave him the Red Hat and called him "My beloved Benjamin". Lisieux and St. Teresa's sisters must be a daily inspiring recollection. What memories there must be, too, of the ruins of Europe, of men and women in despair, of the children in Catholic Poland doomed to slavery of soul and body under the Godless oppressors, of his fellow-bishops imprisoned, tortured, lost! Happily, we may well hope that something of the sufferings of the months of illness have been forgotten, for kindly nature includes such forgetfulness in her work of healing.

As with men who have lived intensely, naturally loving their fellow-men and dedicating their lives to their service, happy memories are mingled with sad ones. The memory of well-earned holidays in Ireland with his closest friend, Archbishop Masterson, is mingled to-day with the sadness of losing that friend, his senior by less than a month, through the sudden onset of fatal illness; "my companion of many years and dearest friend", as he called him in the panegyric which he preached at the requiem in St. Chad's. Recalling holidays in Ireland spent with him, he said on that occasion: "I remember one evening his standing on the shores of Derrynane looking wistfully at the country he loved so well and longingly at the sea. I can see him now [Archbishop Masterson at this time knew of his fatal illness] turning with resignation from this sight and walking quietly to a group of children playing upon the sands. He had never met them before but immediately they captured his own infectious good spirits. He was a man of simple courage."

Remembering that he is now supposed to be taking things more easily, the Cardinal may well surprise himself with the sudden realisation that his latest and freshest memories include something suspiciously like an undiminished activity. Among the journeys which he has made abroad since his recovery, we can number journeys to Rome, as for the canonisation of St. Pius X, and journeys to Lourdes; a journey to Utrecht for the celebrations in honour of the restoration of Holland's Hierarchy; a journey to Spain for the Barcelona Eucharistic Congress; a journey to Germany for the St. Boniface celebrations, he himself having previously been host to German cardinals in this country's celebrations; a journey to Norway to commemorate the eighth centenary of the establishment of Norway's hierarchy by the only English Pope, Adrian IV —on this occasion, he had the pleasure of visiting Norway's King.

Travel abroad, constant travel at home, as he motors through the countryside, quietly saying his Office, always eager to be present in person where Catholics are gathered together in celebration or on a special occasion; the round of diocesan visitations, fitted with difficulty into the round of public engagements, religious and civic; the visitors to Archbishop's House from home and abroad, politicians, diplomats, prelates, priests, laity of all ranks and work; the daily administration of his own diocese; the daily heavy correspondence—all this and much else still falls on his shoulders; this, and much else, is dealt with promptly, decisively, effectively, as has always been his way. And

42 Crowning the statue of Our Lady of Willesden, Marian Year Rally, Wembley Stadium, 3rd October, 1954.

43　With the Holy Father in Rome, June, 1954.

he himself would wish, we are certain, to mention in this connection the devoted work of those who have assisted him in his immense task, of his coadjutor and his auxiliary bishop, of the Vicar-General and members of the Curia of the archdiocese, of the four Selly Park sisters, the order he as Cardinal 'protects', who look after the domestic needs of his household, and by no means least, of his personal secretary, Monsignor Derek Worlock, assisted by Father Anglim. His Eminence would wish, we feel sure, that these pages should not end without a special emphasis on the devotion and work of the priest who is friend as much as secretary, the constant companion of his many journeys abroad, the companion, too, of his continuous travel in this country, ever at hand at home, ever assisting him in his arduous work. The devotion of all who work and live with the Cardinal is, indeed, but the counterpart of the devotion which he himself feels for all those who assist and serve him.

Thus we leave His Eminence the Cardinal relaxing a little at last and quietly musing over the memories and events of his extraordinarily full life. And one memory, surely, remains especially vivid. It is the memory of the young priest of twenty-eight kneeling by the tomb of Cardinal Merry del Val and meditating on the inscription "Da Mihi Animas".

That apostolic call has been the keynote of his whole life. It is the basic explanation of the endless, eagerly-accepted work, done in a spirit of complete submission to the will of God who raised him to his high dignities and responsibilities and who gave him the help of St. Teresa of Lisieux to teach him that, whether for cardinals or the humblest of the human flock, the spiritual quality of each human life lies, not in its importance in the eyes of men, but in the simplicity and spirit of detachment from self-love with which it is lived for the service of God and the spread of His Kingdom.

In health, the Cardinal has given his all for this cause, and the world has had full evidence of the way he has self-lessly laboured through critical times, not only within the limits of his own diocese of which he is Archbishop, or even the limits of his own country of which he is the Catholic leader, but over the world wherein as a prince of the Church his spiritual mission, by the Pope's own direction, ranges. In sickness, the harder test of his self-dedication to the will of God and His service through accepting a share of the suffering of the world is, through his own insistence, less well known. If we have dwelt upon it in these pages, it is because we believe that with him the darker hours are integral with the sunnier ones, affording, moreover, the real clue to the quality and success of his spiritual leadership. His courage and will-power have triumphed over a degree of ill-health that must have over-come most of us, and we pray, hope and expect that, God willing, he may long continue to carry, with the serenity that is always his, the heavy burden which his high dignity, as he sees it, imposes upon him.

INDEX